Also by Brad Schaeffer

Of Another Time and Place
The Extraordinary

LIFE
in the
PITS

MY TIME AS A TRADER ON THE
ROUGH-AND-TUMBLE EXCHANGE FLOORS

BRAD SCHAEFFER

Post Hill
PRESS

A POST HILL PRESS BOOK
ISBN: 979-8-88845-410-7
ISBN (eBook): 979-8-88845-411-4

Life in the Pits:
My Time as a Trader on the Rough-and-Tumble Exchange Floors
© 2023 by Brad Schaeffer
All Rights Reserved

Cover design by Cody Corcoran
Cover Photo: Directphoto Collection / Alamy Stock Photo

Post Hill Press
New York • Nashville
posthillpress.com

Published in the United States of America
1 2 3 4 5 6 7 8 9 10

For

JTS

CONTENTS

AUTHOR'S NOTE

FROM 1989 TO 1994, I was first a clerk then an options trader on the floors of two commodities exchanges: the Chicago Mercantile Exchange and the New York Mercantile Exchange. Those born before the turn of the century may remember them, either from the reportage of cable business channels or being featured in popular films. The equities floors, such as the iconic New York Stock Exchange and American Stock Exchange, where I also briefly traded, were gentlemanly places, in which men in suits and ties serenely bought and sold shares of stocks or options contracts. But the commodities pits, where I cut my teeth, were a seething mass of gyrating, sweaty, type A personalities through whom the nation's commerce coursed as if part of its economic bloodstream. Compared to the hyperfast speed of computers today, open outcry, as it was called, may seem now like an inefficient way to conduct business ... screaming at each other while wildly gesturing in a sign language as unique as this mode of transacting itself. But there was a brutal honesty in how matters were conducted in the trading pits that cut through any pretense. There was also a sense of pride in being one of the working parts of the machine of capitalism itself. We were the ones who made the prices, and took the risk of dealing, either as a buyer or seller, in the commodities that fueled the growth of the United States, and the world, for well over a hundred years.

The commodities exchange floors were at their zenith, in both importance and as a fixture in the national psyche, throughout the eighties and nineties. Trading in the pits was both an exhilarating and intimidating way to spend my day from the opening bell at dawn to the abrupt close of business in the early afternoon. One didn't dress for work in the morning so much as "suit up." In fact, stepping onto the trading floor reminded me very much of running onto the football field while psyching myself up for the big game. The pits of Chicago and New York were uniquely American creations. And, for me, they were without a doubt the most interesting places I've ever worked in my three decades and counting on Wall Street.

But even as the exchanges were reaching their apogee, a shifting under the feet of many of its non-credentialed dealers who, as the saying went, would have been flipping burgers if it wasn't for the floor, was already taking place. Electronic trading was starting to come into its own. And as Moore's Law saw technology grow in exponential leaps of development in ever-accelerating frequency, it became apparent to the more astute observers that the days of the epochal trading floors were numbered. Indeed, they are gone now. And a cherished part of Americana has slipped into the history books.

Life in the Pits was inspired by a suggestion that I should expand upon a 2016 article I wrote for the *Wall Street Journal* entitled "I'll Miss the Trading Floor." And although, like many, I have adapted well enough to the new e-trading world that replaced open outcry in the futures and options transaction process, something in this country died when the exchange floors closed for good. This book is both a record of, and homage to, that unique band of iconoclasts, misfits, and bona fide geniuses next to whom I stood literally elbow-to-elbow every day, eight hours a day. I hope, in my small way, I can keep alive the memory not just of these once-great exchanges, but also those who made them the unique treasures they were.

"Over the past decade, the financial markets have changed too rapidly for our mental picture of them to remain true to life. The picture I'll bet most people have of the markets is still a picture a human being might have taken. In it, a ticker tape runs across the bottom of some cable TV screen, and alpha males in color-coded jackets stand in trading pits, hollering at each other. That picture is dated; the world it depicts is dead."

—MICHAEL LEWIS

⌒

"Greed is a basic part of animal nature. Being against it is like being against breathing or eating."

—BEN STEIN

⌒

"I want an Oompa Loompa ... *now!*"

—ROALD DAHL

CHAPTER 1

RESPECT RISK

JIM BARKHORN WASN'T A RICH man. Certainly not by the standards of the collection of millionaires who surrounded him, pressed up against each other in a tight group shoulder to shoulder. They jostled for position, shoving and elbowing those around them, while nervously talking amongst themselves about what today might bring. Some of the men (it was almost all men) who were wedged chest-to-back as one might imagine on a rush-hour subway car had already made fortunes in this place. Jim aspired to be one of them someday. But, then again, many more had come here only to lose a significant chunk of their net worth in a short period of time and then just disappear, never to be seen or spoken of again. As a saying in this business goes, "Many are called, but few are chosen." Jim had been one of the called. Whether or not he was ever to be among the chosen would depend very much on what happened in the next six hours and forty minutes. All he knew for sure was that as of right now, at the ripe old age of twenty-seven, he stood a very good chance of losing everything.

He wasn't at a casino, leaning against the lip of a craps table praying the upcoming roll wasn't a seven or eleven. Rather, he was standing in a crowded trading pit deep in the bowels of the floor of the Chicago Mercantile Exchange. The CME, or "Merc," as it was simply called, along with the Chicago Board of Trade (CBOT), its sister exchange a few blocks away, was a massive amphitheater in which commodities futures and options were bought and sold in a beehive of screaming, red-faced traders, doing deal after deal in a manner that seems archaic today. Arms flailing, shouting, scribbling down transactions on cardboard trading cards, this place was the epicenter of commerce in which the prices of so many of the products Americans use every day were determined. Meats like live cattle, feeder cattle, and pork bellies. Butter. Lumber. As well as various financial instruments that allowed one to manage interest rate exposure and speculate in the fluctuations of currency exchange rates and equities.

The products Jim traded, Eurodollar options, were among the hottest new offerings from the Merc. Their usefulness in managing interest rate risk had made them a popular outgrowth of the exchange's bellwether product, Eurodollar futures. Eurodollars are what the name implies. US dollars deposited in foreign banks, which are outside the realm of FDIC protection and thus pay slightly higher interest in exchange for the added risk. Like bond futures, Eurodollar futures are used as a hedge against interest rates. As rates rise, the value of Eurodollar futures fall, and vice versa. Also like bonds, when the equities markets show signs of weakness, they are often seen as a safe haven into which money managers can move assets and ride out the storm. And today the stock market wasn't just caught in a squall; it was being battered by a full-fledged typhoon. This was the early morning of October 20, 1987, and for the first time in his two years on the floor, Jim Barkhorn was about to see just how dangerous the markets could be.

Tall and lanky with an affable demeanor, Jim was one of the more well-liked members of the exchange. He was also one of the newest. Coworkers and others on the floor never called him Jim but rather "JEB." This was the three-letter acronym stamped in plain white lettering on the stiff square badge pinned at a cockeyed angle to the lapel of his cherry-red busboy-like jacket. As he stood among the crowding traders, each preparing for what this day portended in his own way, JEB was replaying in his head a conversation he'd had with Bill Gladstone, a long-time veteran of the pits. "GATS," as his badge read, had taken a liking to JEB and so would offer him some well-earned nuggets of knowledge...even as they were technically competitors. But Bill was already rich, and one more trader in his pit wouldn't make or break him. Besides, they might end up doing each other favors in the future.

Whatever his motivation, GATS had grown concerned for the young trader next to him. JEB trusted Bill enough to occasionally let him glance at his options position and assess its potential profits and risk profile. GATS had noticed that the young Barkhorn was starting to trade in lumps of contracts that were very large, indeed too large, for the $200,000 size of his account. He also tried to alert him that his account was vulnerable to an outsized move, especially to the upside. "Don't lose respect for risk," Bill cautioned the newbie. "I've seen this market do crazy things. And it's usually when you least expect it... and are most exposed. It's almost like God plans it that way just to knock our dicks back in the dirt and keep us humble."

JEB thanked him politely, but in the back of his mind dismissed the seasoned trader's concerns as hyperbole. As far as volatility went, if Eurodollars were anything, they were slow, plodding, and at times quite boring. If he wanted the gut-wrenching action that outsiders usually associated with the wild west of the commodities game, JEB thought, he'd be in one of the pits where they traded corn, wheat, or metals... markets that whipsawed up and down like an EKG. Not here. As long as the Eurodollars didn't do anything crazy he'd be able to manage any risk.

But now the veteran's words of warning were hitting Barkhorn in the face. Something strange had happened to the stock market. All day yesterday the traders watched as the Dow tanked. Down 50, then 100, then 200, finally ending what would be known as Black Monday at 508 points down. That was a 22.6 percent hit... far greater than the 12.62 percent crash in October 1929, which ignited the Great Depression. When the Eurodollar traders went home that night, they could comfort themselves in the fact that, although the world's financial markets seemed to be ripping apart at the seams, their stolid Eurodollars barely registered concern.

That had been last night. But by the time JEB walked onto the trading floor this morning something had changed. It was as if the world's money traders had snapped out of their stupor and were finally taking notice. There was a nervous energy on the exchange floor that JEB had never felt before. What was it exactly? Excitement? No. More like anxiety. Panic, even. He stood in his spot, rocking back and forth on his feet as the digital clock above the floor crept toward the opening 7:20 a.m. bell, examining a printout of his trading position and running what-if scenarios through his head. Five points up or down was a pretty decent move in Eurodollar futures overnight. Erring on the side of caution, JEB considered levels beyond that. *If we*

LIFE IN THE PITS

open up ten points higher how will I do? How about ten points lower? How about fifteen even? His clerk, Mitch, came up to him. JEB was splitting his salary three ways with two other traders. Mitch's job was to help the traders keep track of their positions by providing them updated portfolio statements throughout the day while attending to their needs from a request for a new pen to getting them chewing gum. Like a squire to a crew of medieval knights. He wore the distinctive school bus yellow blazer-like jacket the CME required all nonmembers to wear. It was part of the hierarchy of the floor.

"Mitch, what's the call?" Jim asked as he took a stack of fresh trading cards from his clerk's outstretched hand and stuffed them into his pocket. He was asking how much higher or lower the Eurodollars were expected to open relative to yesterday's settlement price.

Mitch looked at him nervously. "Futures are forty higher so far."

"Four higher?"

"No, man. *Forty.*"

JEB frowned at him with incredulity. "Forty? No, that can't be right. Check it again."

Mitch went off to find one of the clerks for the large brokerage houses to double-check. Wherever their big institutional clients' orders were coming in pre-open would indicate the call. He got his answer and returned. "Shit, Jeb," he said. "The futures are called sixty higher now."

Barkhorn was now officially nervous. He had an options position that was safe within an unheard-of fifty-point move either way. But any higher or lower than that and he was what was called "short the wings." What that means doesn't really matter, other than his risk beyond a certain point was open-ended. As GATS had pointed out first thing that morning, Jim's position was vulnerable to a sharp move in the futures to the upside. With any opening above fifty, as the call indicated, JEB would start to really hemorrhage money.

At 7:05 a.m. Mitch said to JEB in a hushed voice, "The call's one hundred higher now." JEB went numb. The market wouldn't open for another fifteen minutes, and the call was moving up in ten-point increments. He was learning what "flight to quality" meant. Money was leaving the cratering stock market in a panic and buying Eurodollar futures in anticipation of a Fed rate cut to try and bail out a soon-to-be heavily-in-recession, if not depression, US economy. Interest rates go down; Eurodollars go up. In this case, a lot.

By 7:15 a.m. the call was 150 higher and still climbing. The young trader was despondent. He'd never felt so powerless. Barkhorn's entire liquid net worth was in his trading account. At home in his Chicago apartment he had a wife and young children who depended on him. And yet, as it stood right now, the moment the Eurodollar futures began trading, JEB was ruined. And there was nothing he could do about it. "In five minutes my life is over," he muttered to himself. Then he took a deep breath, popped a stick of gum in his mouth, and stared up at the ticking clock frowning down on him with cold indifference, waiting in forlorn silence for the opening bell to sound. JEB felt very much like a man calmly taking his last drag on his last cigarette as he stood before the firing squad.

CHAPTER 2

FROM ARTIST
TO YELLOWCOAT

PEOPLE OFTEN ASK ME HOW I became a part of the commodities trading world...that little-known back alleyway in the financial neighborhood. Answer: obliquely. Meaning my first postcollegiate job was as far away from the trading pits of Chicago and New York as one could imagine. But, as Steve Jobs liked to say, sometimes you can only connect the dots backward.

Black Monday was barely two years in the rearview mirror when I drove away from the University of Illinois campus in Urbana-Champaign for good with my BA in Communications in hand. I had no clue as to what I wanted to do from a career standpoint. And I had no idea the commodities business even existed. Once I learned a little bit about it—there were a lot of traders scattered across the Chicagoland area in 1989—I concluded I had no ambitions to relegate my degree to becoming a gopher for crass men with high school educations who said things like "I look at every woman I see" or "How did Lou Gehrig die?" And yet that's exactly what I ended up doing.

The beginning of a journey that would land me in the frenetic trading pits of legend in the 1990s at their pinnacle, and offer me a front-row seat to the excesses, exploitations, hilarity, pain, and even criminality of some of the most lucrative markets most have never heard of, began, oddly enough, in an advertising agency. It was housed in the classic Jewelers Building, a landmark downtown skyscraper at the corner of Wabash and East Wacker Drive, adjacent to the Chicago River. The building was completed in 1927 and supposedly the domed top floor was once the location of Al Capone's favorite restaurant. I often wonder if the ghosts of those raucous hoods—men who drank hard, played hard, and firmly believed neither social mores nor the rule of law had any hold on them—wafted down through the ceiling vents to infiltrate my soul in some sort of preparatory ritual for the life I would lead.

I had always been a decent artist, and even though I never took any formal classes in college I did enough work on my own to piece together a legitimate portfolio. Through the recommendation of a girlfriend's father, who was a partner at a Chicago law firm, I found myself sitting in a sterile conference room with a well-tailored and impeccably groomed creative director of a boutique advertising agency. I nervously watched him as he flipped through my drawings (the subjects included: a positive/negative John Lennon from *The White Album*, Confederate cavalrymen trotting through the snow-covered mountains of Tennessee, and a box of Raisinets, just to name a few). "Mmmm hmmmm…," he would mutter, studying each work as would a jeweler appraising your grandmother's wedding ring. Then he'd turn over the heavy laminated sheet to the next drawing, and a gold cufflink would tap on the shiny oak tabletop like Morse. "Mmmmm *hmmmmm*…." (He liked that one, I guess.) And finally, slamming the portfolio closed, he looked up at me.

"Well," he said, removing his wire-rimmed glasses and polishing them with his silk handkerchief. "Self-taught?" I nodded yes, unsure whether that was a good thing or not. "Mmmm... hmmm. And you say you know Ray Silverman?"

I nodded again. "I know his daughter."

"Becca's a peach, wouldn't you say?"

I would say.

"Well then." He sighed. "Perhaps there's an angel lurking somewhere in this slab of marble Ray sent me. I suppose you'll do."

The following Monday I was perched on a high swivel chair facing an angled art table scribbling pictures of Quaker Oats Chewy granola bars for presentation storyboards. A lot of good four years in college did me. Although I had learned to parallel park, so it wasn't a total loss.

I shared the room with two other artists who were true archetypes of the fiercely independent, creative breed with whom I've always felt a sort of kinship. Kenny had been there, it seemed, since Eisenhower was president. He sported thick glasses, a full bushy gray beard, and a flowing mane of long, wavy hair of the same silvery hue; the running joke was you never saw Kenny and Jerry Garcia in the same room. He was a chain smoker with one proverbial foot in the grave and the other on black ice, and he hacked incessantly in between drags of Camels. The art room's air quality could've given a humid day in Beijing a run for its money. One of my jobs, in fact, was to descend to the lobby every morning and buy him his two daily packs. I was also tasked with running to the packaged goods store a few blocks down State Street under the L train and procuring the required six-pack of Old Style beer, which he slurped regularly throughout the day. For all the sins against his body, Ken was a gifted artist. He had a knack for visualizing what the account execs wanted and bringing their nebulous ideas to life through ink on fifty-pound paper.

The other artist, Gareth, was three years out of Emory. He was clean-shaven, yet wore a ponytail that ran all the way down the small of his back. He reminded me of the actor Tom Hulce, who played Amadeus in the eponymous film. Ken and Gareth both adopted jeans, sandals, and the gaudy Aloha shirt as the official uniform of their little fiefdom. They generally kept to themselves, rarely venturing out of their cloistered art room to mingle. During client presentations, they stood in silence against the wall until directly addressed. They were two of the happiest souls I would ever work with. This seemed like a nice start for me. I thought I might make art a career. But my stint there would only last a few months. The problem with advertising, as they used to say, was that it was a great business to be in if your parents could afford to send you. I would also discover to my disappointment that while I enjoyed being creative for fun or an escape, being a professional artist lost its luster when you had to be creative and/or escapist by four this afternoon or else.

This seems like an odd starting point for a reflection on pit trading. But I embark here, in a business far removed from the mathematical world of derivatives, to drive home two points about how a lifelong career in the commodities markets often germinated.

First, back in 1989 when the trading pits of Chicago ruled, most people found their way down to the floor of either the Chicago Board of Trade or the Chicago Mercantile Exchange—I eventually landed in the latter—via unconventional routes. Sometimes it was pure happenstance. A chance meeting at a bar, maybe. Or perhaps an unsolicited phone call from a frat brother who had a brother in the S&P 500 pit who knew a guy in the Live Cattle pit looking for a clerk. In my case it was pure nepotism, as I'll explain later. The thing was, unlike investment or commercial banking or institutional dealing, there were no commodities-pit recruiters descending upon Urbana-Champaign to shake your sweaty palms and grill you about Friedrich Hayek or Bretton Woods or hand you a marker and challenge you to step up to a grease board and squiggle out the Black-Scholes model used for pricing options. You just graduated college, got your diploma, packed up your meager belongings, aimed the car north for the Chicago area, and trusted fate to do the rest. As such, most people who eventually found their way into the trading pits tended to be opportunists and scrappers for whom tradition and convention were not so much anathema as foreign. They arrived via circuitous paths. In a strange outlier of Darwinism, in most cases only the most inventive, creative, and resourceful people the Midwest's underrated state university system had to offer possessed the chutzpah to get onto the floor...and stay there.

The second reason I bring up my brief stint in advertising is that it was a good introduction to my place in the real world outside the ivy-coated university bubble. And thus the job mentally and emotionally prepared me for what was to come. As with being a new art assistant, in order to survive your first year in the trading pits you had to be willing to check your pride at the door, work long hours, perform the gruntiest of grunt work, and do it all for very low pay. I still lived at my widowed mother's house in the suburbs during my first few months of work, and although the art department had a casual atmosphere, Ken and Gareth were my overlords who demanded all of my time. I learned discipline and how to take instructions from people who didn't give a damn about my degree... one that in no way prepared me for life in their world. In college the earliest class was the dreaded 8:00 a.m.; those days were gone. Now I caught the 5:15 a.m. train to make the forty-five-minute commute to Union Station and then hoof it following the dogleg bend of the Chicago River down Wacker Drive to the office off Wabash Street. Well before "Kenny G," as I called Ken and Gareth collectively, arrived with their bloodshot eyes and burping last night's cheap bourbon, I set up the art room, sharpened the charcoal pencils with the X-Acto knife, cleaned the T squares, made sure we had ample supplies of paper, and brewed a fresh pot of coffee. And in between doing the odd drawings they needed, I was their gopher running several times a day back and forth from our office to the agency's biggest client, Quaker Oats, right across the river. They quickly exorcised any notions of entitlement I might have had.

If I may digress further... I think all the jobs I held before making my way to the Chicago Merc were parts of some master plan to prepare me for having my ego atomized the first day on the floor. My first paying gig at sixteen was doing unskilled labor at an apple orchard a bike ride from my house. One of the more glamorous duties was shoveling compost. In my senior year of high school I was a physical education instructor at a housing community for the mildly to profoundly mentally disabled, and learned to deal with unpredictable, often violent and self-destructive eruptions. Such a position taught me patience and how to cope with irrational outbursts aplenty—in many ways this experience provided the best training of all for dealing with irate traders. In summers during my college years I waited tables at a place that offered itself up as a fine restaurant, but was really just a glorified hamburger joint. But I learned how to work under intense pressure. During the rush as many as five tables, some just couples, others raucous groups of ten, would all be seated in my section at once—I think the hostess liked to overwhelm me as a sadistic flirtation like a grammar-school girl kicks the shin of the boy who strikes her fancy. That's when you had to learn to mentally stack up tables quickly in the correct priority of service: the immediate needs (that all-important calming first round of drinks); those growing impatient (the ones twisting in their chairs and looking around as if expecting to spot their order orbiting the room in midair); then those enjoying *Le Hamburger* and only in need of cursory attention; finally those just waiting for the check. I would find these collating skills of tremendous value to me when the markets exploded and buy and sell orders were fired at me via hand signals from all over the floor.

• • •

It's not farfetched to claim cigarettes changed my life. And the architect of that change was strolling down East Wacker Drive just as I was putting the finishing touches on a sketch of a shiny red box with the word *Magna* emblazoned in diagonal retro-fifties muscle-car chrome along the front. Magna was a new brand of cigarette being proffered by the tobacco merchants of RJR Nabisco, who were one of our clients. Our agency was cynically tasked with making the products appeal to the youth market. Rebellious packaging, flashy, in-your-face prime-colors motif, vivid and vibrant; it was James Dean in a box of cancer sticks.

I had difficulty with this from an ethical standpoint, although I kept my feelings to myself. Kenny G and I never got into politics or anything even close to it. I don't think our views of the world would have jibed very much, and I didn't feel like getting on my bosses' bad sides. But they seemed morally indifferent to a product and a campaign I saw as the equivalent of lining up four hundred thousand kids a year—the number of new smokers needed to replace the ones who died off annually—in front of a firing squad. I'd seen family members suffer from emphysema, strokes, and cancer of the larynx (I had an aunt with a hole in her throat who spoke through a vibrating handheld device that gave her voice a robotic quality). And, with my own teen years still fresh in my mind, I knew how kids felt invulnerable and thus had no idea that the moment they got hooked, the bullets from the firing squad were on the way courtesy of the ad men of New York and Chicago. It would just take some time to hit their mark. Actually, we weren't firing bullets so much as poisoned darts laced with a slowly seeping pathogen.

As it was, I was already getting tired of the advertising life. The hours were long, the pay crap, and the pressure from the accounts people to be creative and have the muse whisper in your ear by this or that deadline was unrelenting. And now we had to sell products that I knew would kill. Sure, RJR's mantra was: "We're not trying to create new smokers, just get a larger piece of the existing market." But we all knew better. Like any business, it was a numbers game. The tobacco industry required a new pledge class every year to replenish its lost customers due to what the methodical British called shellfire casualties in World War I, "normal wastage." By the time I stared down at my handiwork on the table, a very retro-chic cigarette box that even I, a hopeless asthmatic, might want to roll up in my shirtsleeve, I was ready for a change.

Such was my primed mindset when fate came calling.

• • •

The three favorite "isms" on Wall Street are capitalism, cronyism, and nepotism. The first is noble, the second is hypocritical when juxtaposed against the first, and the third is just the way it is. And for the second time in a few months I found that it was who I knew, rather than what I'd learned in four years of undergrad studies, that mattered most.

My older brother by five years was one of those men who could part a crowd like Moses. At six-one, two hundred pounds of pure muscle, and five pounds of defined jaw to go with it, he had *GQ* model good looks. But his aesthetic qualities—chiseled face, military-cropped auburn hair, and infectious smile— were surpassed by his personality, which he had in abundance. He was one of those people who just seemed to have it all and, as the old saying goes, women loved him, and men wanted to be him. I was one of those men.

So, when he showed up in my office with an invitation to lunch, I was eager to get out and about with him. He was dressed in curious garb that at once intrigued me. Besides khakis, a collared shirt, and sneakers, he was wearing a navy blue and teal jacket with several oversized pockets stuffed with rolled-up sheets of paper laden with numbers on one side and what looked like a shallow stack of index cards on the other. He also sported a tie that very well could have come from the Salvation Army, the knot loosened about his chest. A row of pens peeked out of his breast pocket. On his lapels were pinned several buttons for personal flair. One I remember read: "In Search Of The Eternal Buzz." But the most prominent feature was a large, deep blue, roughly four-inch-by-four-inch square pinned to his other lapel. On it were etched in big white Arial font print the letters TBS and below them the number 215.

"To what do I owe the pleasure?" I asked him as his eyes canvassed the art room.

"So this is your office," he said. "Impressive."

"It's not my office," I corrected him. "My bosses are at lunch." Kenny G would be gone for two hours. In fact, this being a Friday, the odds of them returning at all were minimal.

"You like it here?" he asked.

I shrugged. "Pays the bills."

His eyebrows raised and he fixed me with a keen stare. "Does it really?" he said with a skeptical tone that put me on the defensive.

But I dropped my fighting stance and simply offered that it's what I do. "So anyway, what brings you here?"

He smiled and put his powerful hand on my shoulder. "Come with me. I'm taking you to lunch. I want you to see *my* office."

CHAPTER 3

THE FLYING CIRCUS

THERE ARE CERTAIN WATERSHED MOMENTS in life one keeps
with them, like a tattered photograph permanently stuffed in
their wallet. For me, one of them was the first time I stepped
onto the floor of the Chicago Mercantile Exchange...my brother's "office."

What first hit me as we pushed through the darkly tinted
heavy glass doors and the enormous 35,000-square-foot
amphitheater opened up before me was the noise. Even in the
quieter moments of the trading sessions (this was a Friday
afternoon and there were no market crashes to attend to) the
cacophony from some 1,500 agitated voices laid into you like a
blast of exhaust from a city bus. The high-pitched screams, the
gruff shouts, and the hurling of insults and curses all blended
into one unintelligible banshee roar, not unlike the sounds of
an overflow crowd at a World Cup match. The noise assaulted
my ears and made me wonder how anyone could get any business done in this chaos.

Then there was the smorgasbord for the eyes. The clerks all
wore bright yellow jackets no matter who they worked for. They
tended to stand either ringing the outer rims of the pits like pond
brine or manning the ranks of phones and order stations that par-

enthetically bracketed the trading area. But I was really struck by the multitude of colors that the traders and exchange members displayed. They reminded me of the gaudily painted German triplanes in the Red Baron's "Flying Circus" squadron. Beyond the standard-issue ruby-red blazers provided by the exchange, many companies and individual traders preferred their own uniforms. There was the lime green of O'Connor Corp. The olive with crimson trim of Cooper Neff & Associates. The powder blue of Refco, Inc. The teal and navy of my brother's firm, First Global, Inc. Some wore taxicab checkerboard patterns. Others candy stripes like members of a barbershop quartet. A few preferred all black to look menacing. Others opted for the more benign snow white with just a splash of red or orange on the shoulders. And still others had their own unique patchwork, even tie-dyed. Naturally, one of the cattle traders sported the same black-and-white blotched pattern of a Holstein cow. The variety of hues served a utilitarian purpose beyond just expressing individuality or corporate affiliation. It was to distinguish oneself enough to be picked out in the crowd of traders and clerks that could number in the hundreds in the largest pits like the Eurodollar futures at the CME or the Treasury Bond pit at the Chicago Board of Trade a few blocks southeast on Jackson Boulevard.

Even the badges themselves revealed some clues as to the floor's myriad of personalities. There was an older Greek man whose acronym was—what else?—OPA. (One imagines if he could have put an exclamation point at the end of it he would have.) A family of brokers whose roots were in the haberdashery industry before coming to the floor were HAT, CAP, and DRBY. One had the slightly sinister XRAY (as if he could read your mind). A sense of whimsy often played into it as well, as

OHNO, NXS, YME, COOL, and ICU could attest. What letters you chose were actually pretty important because it was usually by these acronyms rather than your name you'd be referred to and remembered. No one ever said, "I saw Mike at the Cubs game," but rather, "I saw CPR at the Cubs game." Everything about the pits expressed a sense of singular identity. It was yet another aspect of the ruggedly independent and entrepreneurial nature of the business.

As for where HAT, OPA, GATS, and the rest spent the majority of their days, the CME trading floor was divided up into individual pits, literally concentric circles of descending Dante-like levels like mini-amphitheaters, each servicing a particular product: Eurodollars, T-bills, S&P 500, live cattle, feeder cattle, pork bellies, and various currencies which included in those pre-Euro days the British pound and German Deutsche mark, along with the Japanese yen, Canadian dollar, Australian dollar, and Swiss franc.

Although from behind the high windows of the observation deck it looked like a disorganized hive, as any apiarist will tell you, beehives are actually well-organized systems, with each buzzing insect carrying out a very defined function. Outside the pits were multitiered rows of desks with spastically blinking phones manned mostly by yellowcoat clerks. They worked for the floor brokers, who were either independent operators or part of larger executing clearing firms or investment banking houses. A customer from anywhere across the world—New York, London, Frankfurt, Hong Kong, Tokyo, and Singapore being the major concentrations outside of Chicago itself— would dial up the phone clerk who would scribble the order down on a special carbon-paper deal ticket and time-stamp it with a loud *ka-chunk*! Then the phone clerk would frantically attract the attention of their specific yellowcoat, called an arbitrage clerk, who usually stood unsteadily maintaining his balance among the shoving and jostling at the outside rim of the required pit. The arb clerk stood with his back to the ring scanning the phone stations awaiting orders. The phone clerk would "flash" with a series of hand signals the order to the arb clerk who would then twist toward the pit and grab the shoulder of the executing broker who stood gazing out over the colorful valley of humanity. Below the broker was a convulsing mass of traders all vying to get a piece of the order—the "paper," as was the slang, referring to the time-stamped sheet. The independent traders, on the other hand, were known collectively as "locals." A typical transaction in the Eurodollar futures pit where I would soon start might go something like this:

> The phone clerk takes the call from, say, Goldman Sachs, time-stamps it, and then waves frantically at his arb clerk who is on the lookout for a hailing from the booth:
>
> **Phone Clerk:** "Hey!" [The arb clerk acknowledges, and the order is "flashed" by hand signals.] *September... Buy... Thousand... Market... Goldman.*
>
> **Arb Clerk:** [Grabs broker and whispers in his ear] "Sep. Buy a thousand. Market."
>
> **Broker:** [Faces pit, arms raised] "Sep! Where's Sep!"
>
> **Traders:** [Flocking to him like a prison guard dispensing bread at the Gulag] "Nine-Oh! Nine-Oh!"

This is shorthand for perhaps 91.89/91.90. Everything is abbreviated and everyone already knows what the full price or "handle" is, so no need to say "ninety-one eighty-nine at ninety-one ninety" when just the nine/zero will suffice. This means the traders, who don't know if the broker has an order to buy or sell, will pay him 91.89 for the September futures or sell it to him at 91.90. They wait to see what he's up to.

Broker: "Nine bid!"

Traders: "At Oh!"

Broker: "Nine bid!"

He's trying to pay "the bid" for his client as opposed to lifting "the offer." But the traders stand firm.

Traders: "At Oh!"

The broker pauses for effect and surveys the outstretched fists aimed at him, the hand signal for "zero," or in this case, "ninety." Tapping the fists of his favored traders directly in front of him he begins fulfilling the order.

Broker: "Buy Two hundred Frankie! Two hundo Betts! Jimmy Two-Hundo! Hundred Vox! Hundo Sandy! Hundo Joey! Hundo Cal! [To clerk] You're filled!"

Arb Clerk: [Hand signaling to booth with a thumbs-up] *"Filled!"*

As my brother escorted me through the aisles lined with yellowcoats and multicolored traders I marveled at the arena aspect of it all, taking in this extraordinary Thunderdome of shoving, shouting, and flailing bodies that were in the overheated core of the unbridled, raw capitalist machine that made America the economic powerhouse of the world. The dusty, shoe-printed hard black rubber surface was littered with discarded trading slips, charts, newspapers, financial tables, and the index trading cards that were to the buyers and sellers in this place as binding as a thirty-page legal contract. I picked one up and examined it. A three-and-a-half-by-five-and-a-half-inch carbon-copy sheet that you tore off like an old credit card slip so you had a duplicate record of your trading. It was a simple matrix; blue on the buy side, turn it over and it was red on the sell side. This was a typical futures trading card. Someone had scribbled in the appropriate boxes "50 ZI MCO 135 94.01 G" but then ran an agitated squiggled line through it as if whatever transaction this coded message represented had been canceled and the card tossed in frustration (or relief) onto the floor.

I turned the card over in my hand to get a feel for it. There was a space for the quantity, expiration month, the buyer/seller and clearing firm number, the price, and the time bracket in which the trade was consummated. The most curious word on it was "CARS." This was how contracts were referred to on the floor of the Chicago Merc. You didn't buy fifty futures contracts; you bought fifty "cars." I was informed by an old guard exchange member that the term was a throwback to the days when one contract represented one rail car loaded with cattle. This anachronism reminded me this was an old exchange, and should I decide to come here I would join a continuum and be part of something handed down by the great capitalists of an earlier America that had spread across the continent like a wildfire of Manifest Destiny.

I felt a sublimity here that belied the casual atmosphere of the work environment. Unlike advertising, where my job was to instill in people a covetous desire for things they didn't need—and in the case of Magna cigarettes, would eventually kill them—thus making my previous job a shallow, almost parasitical pursuit, what went on in this exchange and others like it around the world was not just important, but essential. Here was the grease that lubricated the global economic engine and kept it humming, the epicenter of the complex intercontinental mercantile system. I instantly recognized that what was bought and sold here, tools that allowed farmers to guarantee a price for their crops and ranchers for their heads of cattle, CFOs to plan without fear of interest fluctuations, portfolio managers a way to buy and sell proxy baskets of stocks, were an integral part of not just the US but the global economy. What went on down here in this cavernous hall of red-faced alphas had a real and measurable impact on people's lives. You just had to make sense of it all. Divine the method in the madness.

"Man, how do you figure what's going on here?" I asked my brother, raising my voice to be heard above the din.

"You just do."

Fair enough, I thought.

By the time we left the floor and ended up at the Merc Club, the restaurant and bar overlooking the placid Chicago River, I decided I wanted in.

"Why did you bring me here?" I asked him. He offered that I was good with numbers and that it was a great place to make a pissload of money when you're young. It wasn't as profound a pitch as the way Steve Jobs famously lured PepsiCo executive John Sculley to Apple by asking him if he wanted to "sell sugar water your whole life or come with me and change the world," but for me, with barely a pot to piss in and a window to throw it out, the effect was the same. Did I want to draw death certificates for Big Tobacco all day, or come with him and change my life? Seemed like a no-brainer to me. Leaving advertising for the floor would be my first big trade.

• • •

But before I could change said life, I reminded him, I first needed to get a job with some group on the exchange. Anticipating I'd catch the bug the moment I set foot on the trading floor, my brother already had my interview with his boss lined up for the following week. In the chessboard of life, knowledge may be king, but knowing the right people is the all-powerful queen.

And so, the following Monday at 4:00 p.m. sharp, well after the trading day was over, I made the ten-block trek from the ad agency to 30 South Wacker and the office of First Global Trading, Inc. to meet with the first of many fascinating characters I would get to know in the next decade.

Oscar was still a young man, mid-thirties I believe, although I was never sure. Even though I would eventually stand in the same pit with him for three years, he never talked about his life before trading because trading was all he cared about. It utterly consumed him. I cobbled together his curious biography with scraps of info and fleeting gossip over the next few months. Oscar was a native of Finland, educated in one of London's elite universities, and as a result he came to America with not just an MBA but a rabid streak of Anglophilia. Somehow (and I never did learn the major piece that fits in here) he ended up as a pig farmer in Iowa. Yes, from Helsinki to London to the Bridges of Madison County. It was through this enterprise that he came to understand futures trading. He used pork belly futures to hedge his risk. But it didn't take a guy so adept at spotting opportunity as Oscar very long to ditch the farm and head to Chicago where those proxy pork bellies were bought and sold. I could never see this Scandinavian businessman, his thinning hair so blond it almost matched the off-white pallor of his skin, herding pigs for a living.

Not only was Oscar foresighted, but he was also brilliant. He somehow managed to secure a seat on the CME in pork belly futures, choosing for the acronym on his badge DAG. It was a tribute to someone in his past, although I never found out who. And then it was just a matter of time before this trading whiz discovered the options market, still in its infancy then, and filled with mathematical anomalies that translated into lucrative pricing inefficiencies. And from there he cast his sharp, pale-gray eyes across the growing exchange floor and saw that there was even something more profitable than trading pig futures: trading futures on money itself in the growing Eurodollar pit.

A product of the Marshall Plan that sent dollars overseas in aid as well as increased post–World War II trade, it was really the Russians who gave rise to Eurodollars as a hedging tool in a big way during the Cold War. They sold commodities in dollars but kept those Benjis overseas so the US government couldn't get its hands on them as leverage. Eurodollar futures were priced inversely to interest rates. When rates were at zero, the futures traded at par or 100. When rates were at 8 percent, Eurodollars traded at 100.00–8.00 or 92.00. Each "tick," which was the general term in trading for the smallest increment of price change in any market, was one basis point, 1/100 of a full percentage point, or .01. A move from 92.00 to 92.01 was one tick. Each tick in this particular instrument represented twenty-five dollars.[1] Eurodollar futures were an effective hedge against interest rate fluctuations and thus became a very popular financial product among banks and any major concern that had rate exposure. As DAG had predicted, Eurodollars would in time become the CME's flagship product, with volumes rivaling the enormous bond market traded on the CBOT.

I sat across the table in his Spartan conference room, and he sized me up in a way that would always unnerve me. He was a physically small man with the physique of the Pillsbury doughboy and complexion to match, but he carried with him an air, however slight, of menace. This man was a trader to the core. He ate up data and crapped out profits. Like many seasoned traders, his mind was trained to distill everything down to binary mathematics and whether or not anything was a good or bad trade. If there was an angle to be gamed, he saw it clearly and quickly. The saying was that when ordinary people looked at a circle, they saw no edges...Oscar saw an infinite number of edges. He even gamed his own coke machines. We were charged fifty cents per can. But my brother found an invoice

---

1   Each Eurodollar car was a $1 million notional amount, and the contracts were quarterly. So, the calculation was [$1,000,000 x .25 of a year x .01%] = $25.00. Thus, a tick move was a gain or loss of $25 per car.

showing he only paid thirty-five cents. "Damn, that's just edge number sixty-one for him," my brother said.

By the time I first shook Oscar's hand he was already a multimillionaire with trading operations not just in the Chicago exchanges but also in London and Singapore and soon Hong Kong and, most relevant to my future, New York. He sat down across from me, I in my only decent suit, though slightly ill-fitting and wrinkled, and a red "power tie" that was too thin, and him in khakis, his own fat mismatched tie loosened around the neck, and a mind whirring in five directions at once. I tried to break the ice by offering I felt overdressed as no one else was wearing a suit.

"You're interviewing for a job," he replied sharply. "Of course you should wear a suit."

"It's the only one I own," I confessed. I quickly surmised that his attention span was like a rare bird that lands right in front of your window and if your camera's not at the ready it'll fly off. The last thing he had time for was to sit down with this punk artist and go through the formalities of an "interview" when all he needed to know was that I was my brother's sibling. The only thing I needed to know, besides it's good to wear even cheap suits to an interview, was that I better not screw up, or no amount of DNA would save my ass. He actually said that to me. "Oh, and also, welcome aboard, 'Little Shafe.'" And that would be my nickname during my time on the CME floor. Then he was gone. The bird had flown off…but not before I got the prize-winning snapshot. He went back to making money and I got up and left. The entire meeting lasted but five minutes. That's one thing I admire about traders. They cut through the bullshit. I was Shafe's brother. He liked Shafe. So, I already had the job before I sat down.

I found out later that wearing the suit made a good impression on Oscar. He saw it as a sign that I had no sense of entitlement. That was good. Because in the pits no one is entitled to profits. Every dollar is earned. And I've always felt that no one owes me a living. Certainly not Oscar. But he gave me a shot thanks to a caring brother who saw my potential. Sometimes a shot is all you need in life.

• • •

I left the ad agency in the fall of 1989. I'd been a professional artist, my dream job, for barely three months. When I left, Kenny G seemed to have no cares one way or another—or I caught them on a particularly drunk or stoned day. I could have told them the Quaker Oats building was sliding into the Chicago River and it wouldn't have mattered at that moment. I'm sure I was soon forgotten.

On Monday morning, I boarded the 5:15 a.m. train out of suburbia and headed southwest to begin the next several decades of my life—and one wild ride.

CHAPTER 4

TOSSED INTO THE DEEP END

THE FGT OFFICE OCCUPIED A small, unassuming corner on a high floor of the 30 South Wacker building which, along with 10 South Wacker, was one of the two forty-story towers that stood like sentinels above the massive Merc floor situated between them along the river. The space was just a collection of desks, with Oscar's in the middle, and the small conference room where I'd had my brief interview. The break room was nothing but a sink, a bare refrigerator, and that rigged vending machine. Very unimpressive. But that's because our use to Oscar was down on the trading floor, not lounging around in an office hundreds of feet above it.

After filling out the paperwork, my first task before getting to the floor was to procure a yellow clerk's jacket from Roselyn, the FGT office manager. She gauged my size, handed me a worn coat streaked with pen marks from one of the closets, told me to do up my tie, and sent me on my way down the elevator to the trading floor level. "What do I do when I get there?" I asked her. She told me to just look for the Eurodollar pit. Someone named J. R. would take it from there. He was the senior arb clerk. He would be my mentor and would also become one of my best friends.

Once on the floor, I weaved my way through the sea of bodies until I eventually found J. R. It was already 7:10 a.m., just ten minutes before the opening bell would initiate another day of trading futures and options on billions' worth of overseas dollars. The Eurodollar options and futures pits were adjacent to one another. The options pit was constructed as a series of descending concentric levels. It was already overflowing with multicolored traders, like an agitated flock of rare tropical birds, elbowing for position to get close to the brokers on the top step who were their lifeblood. The pit was so packed with traders, brokers, and yellowcoats that I had to physically shove my way through like someone deep inside a sardined train car muscling his way to the exit door before he missed his stop.

J. R. (a Troy Aikman clone) was in his usual position, right where the options and futures pits met. The first thing I noticed about the Eurodollar futures pit was that it was much bigger than the options. It was the size of a decent backyard, and whereas the options pit was more or less octagonal, the futures pit was an enormous rectangular structure which, when viewed from above, was the shape of a coffin. The packed bodies together shifting and pushing to get the best positions took on the character of a heaving mosh pit. It seethed with humanity. The same layered configuration applied. But this pit was utterly huge. The first question of a thousand I would ask the ever-patient J. R., whose mellow southern Illinois country drawl belied his wit and intellect, was why were we standing in this particular spot?

The way it worked, he explained to me while organizing his blank trading cards on which he would take notes, was like this. He was tasked with watching three FGT options traders, strategically positioned triangularly in spots to cover the order flow coming from the brokers on the top step, regardless of from which direction the orders hit the pit. My brother (TBS) was down one level and over to the left. His partner, Max (MAX), a squat, tanned man with flowing black locks not unlike Gareth's at the ad agency, was almost directly in front of us. Oscar (DAG), given his seniority in the floor pecking order, had a spot on the coveted top step to the right, standing next to and at eye level with the most powerful broker in the pit, Zack, whose acronym was ZOF. On the face of a clock, as we were standing on the bottom facing twelve o'clock, Oscar was at one o'clock high, my brother ten o'clock low, and Max seven o'clock low. Our job was to watch them carefully and be ready for any futures orders they would flash to us.

To better understand our particular role, I need to get into the weeds of futures and options trading very briefly. The actual commodities themselves were not exchanged on this floor, but rather various types of financial contracts to buy or sell them. A futures contract is a deal which, as the name suggests, gives one the right to buy or sell a specific standardized amount of a product at a set price sometime in the future, regardless of where the prices may be when the contract comes due. If you're a CFO for a trucking company, for example, and you fear that the price of gasoline a year from now will be higher than today and thus make your operations more costly, you might buy an unleaded gasoline future that guarantees the price you will end up paying when the contract comes due, even if a gallon of gas costs more by then. If, on the other hand, you're a refiner and you're afraid that gasoline prices will fall during the year, thus cutting into your profits, you sell an unleaded gasoline future, and if in a year from now gas is cheaper the buyer of your contract still has to pay today's higher price. What the exchanges did was act as a clearing house, a middleman, by guaranteeing the contracts for a fee while providing an orderly way to keep track of the thousands of such transactions every day. In this example, should either company, the trucking firm or the refiner, be insolvent when the deal comes due, the other side doesn't get stiffed as the exchange is the counterparty and thus is on the hook. Pretty simple, really.

An option on futures takes this concept and makes it three-dimensional and far more complex. Checkers becomes chess. An unleaded gasoline call option expiring in, say, twelve months gives our trucking company the right, but not the obligation, to buy gasoline at the price of the call, or "strike price," a year from now. If at expiration the price of gas is higher than the strike price, or "in-the-money," the buyer of the call will "exercise" the option and take delivery of the gasoline at the predetermined cheaper strike price. If the price of gasoline in a year is lower than the strike price, or "out-of-the-money," the buyer just lets the option expire worthless. This means that, unlike futures that present unlimited risk, when you buy an option, you can only lose what you initially pay for it, called the "premium," nothing more. Such heads-I-win-a-lot/tails-I-lose-a-little contracts aren't free. That's why the option seller charges you for this right. His risk/reward is reversed. The most he can make is the initial premium he collects if the option expires out-of-the-money. If on the expiration date, however, the option is in-the-money (gasoline futures are trading at $3.00/gal and you own a $2.50/gal call, for example) and thus exercised, the seller of the option has to sell gas at that bargain strike price no matter how high gasoline is currently trading. Thus is the seller faced with limited reward but unlimited risk. A put option is the exact same concept, just on the bearish side. A put buyer is betting the market will go lower, the seller higher. The mechanics are more or less the same.

More often than not, option sellers end up keeping all the premium when their shorts expire worthless. Like an insurance company that writes a policy the insured never needs. But on those occasions where markets go ballistic and his short options go deep in-the-money (short calls and the market goes lunar, or short puts and the market falls out of bed) he could lose a significant amount of money. This is why we say that selling options is "like picking up pennies in front of a steamroller." Needless to say, the mathematicians, some of whom I would soon stand beside and marvel at their ability to process lightning-fast calculations in their heads, turned the options market into a casino of probabilities and ever-more-intricate strategies.

When you traded Eurodollar options, if, for example, you bought a call, which gave you the right to buy Eurodollar futures at the predetermined strike price, at a predetermined expiration month (back then they were March, June, September, and December) you were often not just making a bullish bet per se. What made options so attractive to traders, the reason they would spend thousands per month to lease a seat to be on the exchange floor when they could buy or sell options through a broker from anywhere on the globe, was the fact that on the floor they were sold at a slight discount or bought at a slight premium to fair value in return for the liquidity the floor provided. Therefore, a floor options trader didn't care about the future direction of the market as much as he cared about the small mispricing of the options directly in front of him.

For illustration, (using calls for simplicity) if Oscar was asked by ZOF, "Sep ninety-three calls!" Oscar would look up at the futures and see the September futures market trading, say, 92.00. His pricing model as shown on a series of paper printouts in his hand called "sheets" would tell him that at that moment, with the futures trading at 92.00, ZOF's 93.00 calls were worth perhaps 20 ticks. So, DAG would shout above the din: "Nineteen at twenty-one!" He made a market, not knowing if ZOF had an order to sell or buy them. The "Bid/Offer" then was 19 ticks at 21 ticks. If ZOF had an order to buy the calls, DAG would sell them at 21. If Oscar was compelled to buy from ZOF, he would pay 19 for them. If ZOF sold one thousand to DAG at 19, then Oscar's sheets might also have told him that, since he priced the calls against 92.00, he had to hedge them by selling a certain number of futures at that price to theoretically lock in his tick profit. Consider, whenever he bought a call, it was a bullish play. So, to protect himself against falling prices, which would decrease the value of the calls, Oscar would sell futures against his call buys. How many futures he sold depended on what his model said. It was called the "delta" of the option. This gets into more complex finance based on how many days before the options expire, perceived market volatility, and the like, so just trust me on this.[2] So, if Oscar bought a thousand Sep 93.00 calls and his sheets showed him a delta of .30, then for every hundred calls he bought he had to sell 30 futures. And he needed to get the futures sales off at 92.00 or better; otherwise the trade would not be profitable.

---

2   These values came from the earlier mentioned Black-Sholes model, commonly used throughout Wall Street to price options.

That's where J. R. and I would come in....

We'd watch Oscar flailing and screaming at ZOF and then gesturing to us, flashing a hand signal while shouting, "Sep? Sep?!" He wanted to know what the bid-offer was on the September futures trading in the big pit behind us. A broker standing right next to us facing the futures pit who worked for Oscar as FGT's exclusive broker got us the market. His name was Calvin; his badge was CAL, so we just called him "Cal." J. R. grabbed the burly Chicago Italian with a classic mullet and shouted, "Cal! Sep! Sep!" Cal then leaned in toward the mob and screamed, "Sep! What's here?!" The traders milling about in the levels below him all shouted, "Oh bid at One! Oh–One!" That was shorthand for 92.00 bid at 92.01. So J. R. would flash to Oscar, "Oh-One!" He did this by presenting his fist to Oscar knuckles out (zero) and then rotating his wrist 180 degrees and making a gesture like "We're number one." Fist in–zero bid; index finger up and out–at one. Therefore, 92.00 at 92.01. Oscar then patted himself on the top of the head. This, to J. R., meant "What's the size?" Meaning how many were bid for and how many were offered? It made no sense to buy a thousand options that would require a sale of 300 futures on the bid of 92.00 if there was only one guy bidding for one hundred. "Cal! Size! Size!" yelled J. R. above the din of hundreds of screaming voices. Cal demanded from the futures pit: "How many?" Traders screamed at Cal. "Hundred up!" (Meaning he'd buy a hundred or sell a hundred as needed.) "Three hundred by a hundred!" "Five hundred up!" and so on. Cal informed J. R. that there was ample liquidity for Oscar to hedge whatever September expiry option transaction he was considering whether he needed to buy or sell futures. J. R., an experienced clerk, also peered into the pit and confirmed this for himself.

J. R. then faced Oscar and flashed the message: "Size up!" With this information Oscar turned to Zack and bought a thousand Sep 93.00 calls for 19 ticks. We couldn't tell what Oscar was doing, but given his scarlet face, gyrations, and intense expression, we knew he'd just entered into a rather risky trade. We watched closely. Suddenly he flashed with three fingers then balling a fist to his forehead—"Sep sell 300!"—and J. R. turned to Cal and shouted, "Cal, sell three hundred!" We then heard Cal shouting, "Sold Tommy hundred. Hundred Mikey. Hundred Steve-oh!" then to J. R., "You're filled three hundred at oh!" J. R. then gave Oscar a thumbs-up, the flash signal for "filled," meaning the order was fully executed, or fulfilled. Oscar pumped his fist in triumph. He had just made, on paper, $25,000. (One tick profit on a thousand.) All of this took place in a matter of ten seconds. Then it was on to the next trade. Of course, just as easy as it was to make this profit, the market could be cruel. It could also go against you in the worst way if the futures made an adverse move while consummating the options trade, denying you your hedge, and forcing you into a net loser.

So that would be my job. Watch J. R. until I figured it out enough to start taking orders, and ask lots and lots of questions. After trading hours the Merc sometimes offered classes on arb clerking, which included a session of "mock trading" where we all stood around in one of the empty pits like excited children and pretended to deal with each other, doing our best hollering, just to get a feel for the process. Boot camp for yellowcoats. Then I'd go home and practice the complex sign language that brought order to the apparent chaos of the trading pits. I spent my nights literally standing in front of a mirror going over the hand signals until, like a song on an instrument practiced over and over again, the motions were committed to finger memory to the point where they became a second language to me.

For the next several months I stood in that same spot among the crowd from 7:20 a.m. to 2:00 p.m., five days a week. The days began with the 5:15 a.m. train into Chicago and trotting to 30 South Wacker, where I would grab a quick coffee at the FGT office before donning my yellow coat and descending to the trading floor. By 7:00 a.m. I was in my position between the Eurodollar futures and options pits alongside J. R., bumping with the other arb clerks for the best positions from which to view our three options traders who would soon be frantically flashing us orders.

Already the common pre-open question, "Whaddya think here, up or down today?" would be bounced around. The increasing energy of those minutes before the opening bell waiting for the giant analog clock to strike 7:20 a.m. was so palpable you could scoop it out of the air and swallow it. There would be the usual flashing of the letter "C" from traders asking me, or whoever caught their eye, what was "the call," or where was the market expected to open? If I flashed a three and thumb up it meant 3 ticks higher from settle, so if the futures settled the night before at 91.95 the first print was expected to be 91.98. Three and thumb down meant 91.92. A neutral waved hand meant "unch" (unchanged or 91.95). The murmur and kinetic activity of the now filled-to-overflowing trading pits would continue to swell until by 7:19 and thirty seconds the buzz was already starting to fill my ears.

I noticed just before the opening bell would sound that several traders had their own ritual expressions. These were mental exercises to flush the mind of any superfluous thoughts other than the numbers already churning in their heads as they prepared to rapidly solve problems resembling lightning algebra, knowing the slightest miscalculation could cause financial discomfort. One trader always shouted just as the day was about to officially begin: "Time to make the donuts!" My brother liked the *Hill Street Blues*, "Let's be careful out there!" Oscar had my favorite: "Oh, Lawd, won'tcha buy me!"

At precisely 7:20 a.m. the bell rang, and all hell broke loose. There'd be an explosion of screams and shouts, followed by futures orders from all sides flashed at us as if we arb clerks were suddenly ambushed by a crossfire of invisible volleys of money. We'd have to intercept, collate, prioritize, and forward the orders to our brokers to fill as quickly as possible. If the futures orders from Oscar, my brother, or Max were hedges for options trades that expired in months further out on the calendar from the nearest term, or "front-month" where J. R. and I clerked, we'd say they were out on the "futures curve." When these orders came in, we'd then have to turn and flash them to another FGT arb clerk stationed across the expansive sea of bodies on the opposite end of the long rectangular futures pit. He stood nestled in the crowd like a lone sentry way out there in the "back-months" watching us carefully. He would take our flashed orders visually (he couldn't hear us, of course, and could barely even see us) and then flash them again to Jaimo (JAM), our back-months trader and Cal's order-filling counterpart. It wasn't always easy getting JAM's clerk to look our way, and with each passing second as we frantically waved our arms trying to get his attention to flash him the buy or sale, the market could adversely move against the options trader's deal, turning a profit into a loss. One day, J. R. had a particularly difficult time trying to communicate with our back-months clerk who seemed to be spacing out. In exasperation he shouted, "Dammit, what motion do cross-eyed people see?" As you can imagine, as with any passed-along information, each step from trader to clerk to clerk to filling broker offered a greater chance for miscommunication and errors…especially over such distances wherein everything was visual. As I would learn to my horror one day.

And so, another trading day on the floor of the Chicago Merc would be underway.

CHAPTER 5

CHARDONNAY DAYS

ONCE THE INITIAL FRENZY OF controlled chaos following the opening bell subsided, the markets settled into a sort of steady rhythm. The thunderous roar would soften, replaced by a quieter hum like the noise from the stands at a scoreless baseball game at the top of the fifth. As the other pits on the floor opened—S&P 500 at 7:55 a.m., the Meats at 9:05 a.m.—the sudden crescendo of sound again ripped through the air...as one might imagine the spontaneous uproar of a drunken brawl erupting in the bleachers behind you might resonate. Despite the appearance of constant activity, often as not there wasn't much to do. The pits tended to get busy in swells as the prices moved to certain key points, prompting traders to start transacting. But then there were the periods where the markets stayed locked in a very rigid price range, drifting lazily up and down between chart levels of support (floor) and resistance (ceiling) with no real news to jar them into making a significant move. Richard Dennis, a commodities trading legend who started with $400 and earned the first of many millions by his mid-twenties, offered that he made 90 percent of his money on just 10 percent of his trades. That's because markets don't always present clear opportunities like the full-blown equities crash in 1987 or the Nasdaq implosion of 2000, the Hurricane Katrina energy price spike in 2005, the 2008 housing bubble collapse, or the artificially imposed deep recession of 2020 in response to the COVID pandemic.

As such, we often found ourselves trapped in the tedium of mind-numbing lulls in between real trading frenzies, some of which lasted for days as traders awaited the next significant batch of data that might signal which direction interest rates, and thus Eurodollar futures, were headed. We weren't permitted to sit on the trading floor, and it was amazing how long standing on my feet for seven hours straight could feel, even to a hardy twentysomething's spine, despite being permitted to wear comfortable sneakers. I marveled at the stamina of the older traders who stood erect the entire day never even breaking for lunch (no food allowed either) as my much-younger back burned with fatigue and I found myself bending forward with a groan to stretch it out or squatting down like a baseball catcher to get the blood flowing through my legs. During such dead periods, the traders liked to sing the R.E.M. song about standing in the place where you work.

With so many hyperactive minds in one place needing stimulation it's not surprising that the quiet moments on the floor saw episodes of hijinks and mischief to pass the time. The most common gag was to take a heavy cardboard trading card, rip it diagonally into a right triangle, fold the shortest side up a half-inch like a platform, and tear a slit into it. When an unsuspecting yellowcoat walked past you—the clerks were almost always the butt of the jokes, rarely the traders, as was the pecking order of the exchange—you tried to slip the card into the folded lapel collar of the coat at the middle of the shoulder right behind the head. If you did it right, the yellowcoat would be walking around the floor with a cardboard dorsal "fin" jutting from his back. One knew when this particular gag was going down because suddenly there would be cries of "Shark! Help, shark! Everybody out of the water!" The only person unaware of why everyone was screaming like Chief Brody was the poor sap with the fin on his back. Some would walk around the floor for five minutes until eventually putting two and two together and figuring out that the screams of terror were following them around.

During my first week I was "Dino-ed." This was an elaboration of being finned and was usually reserved for greenhorns. The idea was to staple together several fins in a row—four, five, six, as many as would run down the length of a man's back—and then insert the top fin behind the neck again. So now the unsuspecting mark had an entire serrated vertebrae running down his back. Then someone would come up and ask: "Hey, Lil' Shafe, you ever watch *The Flintstones*?" Of course, I'd say. "What's that sound that Dino their pet dinosaur makes again?" And I would do my best high-pitched "*Berp-berp-berp-berp-berp-berp!*" Dino while standing there with dinosaur scales on my back surrounded by yellowcoats and traders all howling with laughter. Fool me once….

"Bombing" someone was another way to liven up a dull day. The idea was to take a golf ball-sized wad of chewed gum—the only edible material allowed on the trading floor, which the edgy traders and clerks munched by the pound—and stick it to one half of a trading card. The card was then folded in two over the wad of goo, a sort of gum taco. Then the card was unfolded again, with the gum now spread across the entire surface like peanut butter. Once "armed" the gum bomb was placed strategically on the floor, gum side up. Now it was just a matter of watching and waiting. It was always fun to see the pack of yellowcoats mingling in the general vicinity of the landmine at their feet. When you saw someone abruptly stop in his tracks and glare down at his now-sticky shoe in consternation the observers would all yell: "Boom!" Gum bombs were a bitch to get off the soles of shoes, as was the idea.

The Tic Tac–eyeglasses gag was always fun to pull on a newbie. Unlike the more malleable candy containers today, back then the little cigarette-lighter-sized Tic Tac boxes were made of thin, rigid plastic. As such, they could be crushed into shards underfoot, producing a very audible and distinct cracking sound that the rubber surface somehow seemed to amplify. The idea was to ask a neophyte, "Hey, lemme see those glasses. I love the frames." When the unsuspecting clerk handed them over, the jokester would pretend to clumsily drop them to the floor (in the jammed mob you couldn't tell he'd palmed them) and then while acting as if he was searching frantically for them in the pushing crowd he would step on a Tic Tac box he'd laid at his feet, making a loud *crrruunnch*! For a few seconds the mark would have to contemplate finishing out his day blind and would briefly panic before he was reunited with his intact glasses while offering a string of expletives in return.

Just because markets could be slow and listless, it didn't stop trading per se. There was constant gambling going on. One trader, a Harvard man, carried a pencil with a tiny set of dice under a plastic dome at the tip where the eraser would be, thus becoming the croupier of a mini craps game going down when time dragged.

Betting pools were always circulating. One clerk collected $500 just for agreeing to get on all fours and eat an entire can of cat food snuck onto the floor. As he was forcing it down with eyes tearing, I heard a trader offer: "I'll throw in another hundred if he drinks a saucer of milk with that."

The most lucrative standing wager had to do with a toupee that was the talk of the exchange. In a stunning deficiency in self-awareness one of the more successful brokers sported a rug so poorly crafted and fitted it looked as if a tribble from the *Star Trek* series had climbed up his back and made a home on the top of the oblivious man's head. But as he filled so much institutional paper that to insult him would effectively cut a trader off from some of the juiciest order flow on the floor, they all just had to stare at that lid all day without saying a word. To him, at least. "His wife lets him go out with that pelt on his head?" and, "You think there are eggs up there?" were comments mumbled amongst the crowd when he was out of earshot. It didn't take long to monetize the floor's fascination with the fuzzy wig. A standing bet was the "Drop the Top" challenge. To wit, how much money would it take for someone to muster the courage to step up to the man and rip the piece off his head? By the time I left the CME, the kitty had grown to five figures. But no one wanted to commit career suicide, so it would remain uncollected, the cranial carpet happily staying in place.

My brother, who in another life could easily have been a writer for *Seinfeld* or *The Simpsons*, had his own ways of combating the ennui of tepid markets. A man whose mind was always racing at Mach speed, he would ponder the wealth gushing all around him and through him and marvel at what a strange unearthly place was the trading floor. He especially got a kick out of the well-groomed yellowcoats with their precisely parted hair and wire-rimmed John Lennon glasses who nevertheless blared on their Walkmans hardcore inner-city rap music ("Damn It Feels Good to Be a Gangsta"). He'd shake his head in amusement at the notion they could've had even the remotest connection to the thug life this genre brought home to underprivileged kids who genuinely struggled to survive in the ghettos of Cabrini Green or the Robert Taylor housing projects, far removed from the obscene wealth of this place.

As such, when the days dragged on and the markets drifted aimlessly with low volumes, my brother concocted a farcical alter ego rap star whose musical offering would better capture the daily struggles of suburbia. The milquetoast rapper character he conceived became known across the floor as "Manila Folder." My brother soon developed an imaginary repertoire of songs that more closely relayed the trials and tribulations of the world in which these kids from Chicago's north shore or Lake County horse country grew up. These songs included: "Chillin' at the Condo Watchin' *Friends*," "Late for My Tee Time," "Chardonnay Days," "Horse Farm in the Hood," and "Don't Be Dissin' My Lawn, Bitch." If idle hands are the Devil's workshop, idle minds on a trading floor were a gold mine of levity.

With this many mostly young men all crowded together, even with proper ventilation a virtual cornucopia of odors drifted over the pits like a morning fog. Fridays were especially interesting because for the traders and clerks Thursday was really Friday to us, and we went out hard in Chicago back then. Very often the clerks had second jobs as bartenders or bouncers to supplement their miniscule incomes. J. R. was a bartender at Mother's, the Division Street bar made famous by the film

About Last Night. The guys who moonlighted as club bouncers tended to be the biggest clerks—including ex-college and even a few pro football players—who'd been hired so they'd be more visible in the pits and could protect a valuable piece of floor space with old-fashioned brute force.

So Thursdays were hard nights, but Fridays were harder days. If you've ever considered placing yourself in a gigantic hangar with over a thousand hungover twenty- and thirty-somethings I would like to dissuade you. Farts were constantly being blasted about the trading floor like the scattered eruptions of sulfur fields and it was easy to see where the gas bombs detonated. A small clearing would open up in a specific area of the pit as those nearest the fart's ground zero suddenly retreated several steps back, like a dilating pupil. From across the pit one could see a rather proud man, the obvious culprit, standing arms folded in triumph in the middle of a ten-foot diameter space all to himself…this on a floor where fistfights might break out over a shifting of a yard here or there.

At least we had a sense of humor about it. One time in the floor bathroom someone had crapped a big, thick, coiled log so monstrous it rose out of the bowl higher than the toilet rim. It was unflushable. Not to be embarrassed by his offering to the porcelain god of the party life, the proud parent left a generic trading card sticking out of the Jurassic turd. On the card was scrawled the challenge to "Top This."

CAL one Friday morning stepped into the pit looking particularly haggard, as if he'd just gone a few rounds with Mike Tyson in between shots of Don Julio. "Tough night, Cal?" I asked. "Oh man," he groaned, "like ya read about, Lil' Shafe."

One broker, it appeared, had partied so hard the night before at one of our local watering holes called The Lodge that he actually fainted and fell forward into the options pit, eventually flopping down onto the bottom-level floor among the discarded trading cards, gum bombs, Tic Tac boxes, candy bar wrappers, balled Kleenexes, and the general detritus from the traders who were nothing to him at this moment but a forest of shuffling pants legs and sneakers. What struck me was not that the man collapsed. Pale pasty wan figures roamed the floor on Friday morning, each with his own regrets and stories to tell from the night before. What struck me was how no one made a move to help him or even cast more than a cursory glance down at him. But I will say the guy was a professional. While lying on his back half-conscious he had the presence of mind to spot through the crowd above him his clerk who was gawking down at him mouth agape and giving the thumps-up: "You're filled ...," he gasped and then laid back and groaned. Eventually one of the pit reporters who monitored the activity like referees summoned for the medical personnel to come in and remove him like a body being evacuated from the battlefield to a MASH unit. The traders grudgingly made room for the EMTs to reach the fallen man. It turned out that the flu and dehydration, not excessive partying, was the culprit in his case. If you're wondering why someone would come into such a work environment suffering from a virus that wiped out fifty million people in a 1918 pandemic, it made perfect sense to us. We even admired his grit. As far as we were concerned, a simple bug was no reason to stay in bed and leave money on the table.

As per the widely proffered cliché, some men actually did suffer bona fide heart attacks. Legend has it that one gray-haired dealer in the S&P futures pit keeled over from a coronary right in the middle of trading. Once his convulsing body lying at the bottom of the pit was noticed, the EMTs were called while the ragdoll of a man was shown all due sign-of-the-cross reverence by traders who were genuinely shocked and concerned. So concerned, in fact, that a few knelt down beside him as he slipped into unconsciousness like the famous painting of General Wolfe at Quebec and made sure he was comfortable and propped his head up and the like. They also managed in the chaos to rifle through his pockets and fill out some of his trading cards before the paramedics arrived to wheel him off the floor to the waiting ambulance. Fortunately, he made a full recovery. His account wasn't so lucky. During the following morning's reconciliation, the hospitalized man's clearing firm noticed that many counterparties from all over the pit were coming in to him with trades showing that he'd either sold them the absolute lows or bought from them the highest highs of the previous day's trading range. It was an expensive episode for him, well beyond the medical bills. When his clerk saw the losses, he supposedly whistled: "Dang, that'd buy a lot of deep-fried Twinkies!"

Yes, Fridays were interesting, and revolting, and sometimes the longest days given the pall of odors from farts and booze residue and garlic stench seeping through tens of millions of sweaty pores, and the burps and breath at such close quarters could be truly horrific. But there was one exception to this Friday hell rule. That was the first Friday of every month. This day was when the previous month's unemployment figure was released. There was no better measure of the health of the US economy than the employment status of the workforce, and thus it was the most anticipated data from which to divine any possible future Fed actions, which, of course, directly impacted price action in the Eurodollars. Thus was this the most important of all the "numbers" of the month ("number" being slang for an impending announcement and flashed by making a "#" with the index and middle fingers of each hand crossing over one another). Traders and clerks were expected to be at their sharpest, so the bars and clubs could wait one more night.

The unemployment figure was released at 7:30 a.m., just ten minutes after trading began, and there was usually a subdued murmur as we awaited the number. Then the announcement would race across the screen:

> -- For the month of November 1989 the U.S. economy added 96,000 new jobs, down 181,000 from the 277,000 reported for October 1989... unemployment held steady at 5.4% --

If the number was close to what was expected, not much happened and it was labeled a "non-event"; the week was effectively over. If, however, unemployment was significantly higher than expected, then that could signal a potential recession down the road, which might prompt the Fed to cut rates to stimulate the economy and futures would rally. If the unemployment was too low, then an economy kicking into high gear could signal rising prices—more people working meant more paycheck cash was out there to buy consumer goods and so vendors could charge more, making each dollar, in effect, less valuable. The Fed might be prompted to raise rates to head off this inflation by making money more expensive, so to speak. Eurodollars might then sell off. This analysis was processed and acted upon before the last digit even ran across the screen, and if there was any significant derivation from the expected number the pit would explode with activity. Often one's week was made—or lost—in the five minutes after the data was released. Needless to say, if there was a surprise you were ill-positioned for, bad things could happen, as I would discover to my dismay soon enough.

CHAPTER 6

SHUT UP AND DANCE

THE MOST POWERFUL BROKER IN the Eurodollar options pit was a gangly man with Hubble lens glasses named Zack... ZOF from my earlier example. What gave Zack his power was that he "filled paper" (executed institutional client orders) for all the major investment banks. Because of his order flow, he was Oscar's most common counterparty, with Oscar strategically perched right next to him as one of the few traders rather than filling brokers to occupy the coveted top step of the pit. They were the most unusual bedfellows. Zack liked Oscar, but I could never tell if Oscar really liked Zack or not. I think he did, as much as a man like Oscar could like anyone. I couldn't see them ever going camping together if Zack stopped feeding Oscar money or Oscar wasn't there to provide accurate markets and enough capital behind them to allow Zack to quickly fill large orders for his biggest clients who valued speedy, seamless execution above all else. Good service brought more business, and more business meant better service from Oscar. Even though they'd yell and scream at each other like old hens, calling each other names from "whore" to "thief," the relationship was symbiotic. They were very much like the old *Looney Tunes* cartoons featuring Ralph Wolf and Sam Sheepdog who met each morning in a meadow and would begin their nine-to-five "jobs," which entailed the former trying all day to steal a sheep under the nose of the latter guarding the flock. They'd greet one another with a cordial "good morning" as they punched in and had their morning coffee, but when the whistle blew they'd proceed to beat the tar out of each other. Paradoxically, they'd share a drink and sandwich during the lunch break in between the severe poundings and even wish each other goodnight as they went home for the evening, only to show up to go at each other all over again in the morning. Oscar summed up their odd friendship this way: "It's hard not to like someone who gives you money every day."

Still, Zack and Oscar would often have heated words throughout the course of the day. Usually they stemmed from Oscar's frustration at the broker "jamming" him with trade after trade. Meaning he kept forcing Oscar to buy more and more of the same option at lower and lower prices (or sell at higher and higher prices if ZOF's customer was a steady buyer) thus making DAG's first batch of ZOF's relentless series of trades automatic losers. In the end, Zack didn't work for Oscar. He worked for his institutional clients. And if it took occasionally decapitating his favorite market-maker to get Goldman Sachs or Morgan Stanley or Deutsche Bank the best fills possible so be it. An angry exchange might go something like this.

> **ZOF:** "March fifty calls?! I need a market on three hundred!"
> **DAG:** "Ten-eleven! Three-hundred-up."

ZOF: "Sold! What's the follow?" (Asking for a new market on the same calls.)

DAG: "Follow? I thought you just needed three hundred?"

ZOF: "Come on, Oscar, what's the follow? This one'll clean me up."

DAG: "Nine bid for three hundred. If it cleans you up."

ZOF: "Sell you three hundred!"

DAG: "Fine."

ZOF: "March fifty calls! Where are they now?"

DAG: (Growing furious.) "Where are they *now*? Let me guess. You have more to sell after all. Zack, should I just drop my pants and bend over for you?"

ZOF: "I just need three hundred more. Really."

DAG: "Bullshit. You've been jamming me like this all day."

ZOF: "No, I swear, Oscar. This time I'm not lying!"

Since the floor brokers did have the power to make or break a trader's career by choosing to whom they could dish out the deals with the most value, they were wined and dined by those same traders on a regular basis. (A power structure that would be reversed in the over-the-counter world.) Thusly would my brother and Max find themselves out until all hours of the night with ZOF or some of the other top-step brokers who were all too happy to run up Oscar's Amex platinum card. ZOF loved nothing more than clubbing, whereas my brother and his partner were more fond of sidling up to one of Chicago's more down-to-earth pubs and whiling the night away. Oftentimes, when they'd find themselves on a strobe-lit dance floor while ZOF and his entourage of clerks gyrated to the "*Ummm-tsss! Ummm-tsss! Ummm-tsss!*" beat of some trendy DJ's rhythms, my brother would shout over the din to Max, "Is making an extra forty ticks a day really worth all this?" To which Max would holler back, "Just shut up and dance!"

At the time, Zack was a man who struck me as consumed by money. But with the passage of many years, I see things differently. Zack just understood what Beatrice Kaufman once observed: "I've been rich and I've been poor, and believe me, rich is better." In fact, a lot of people I once self-righteously labeled as greedy, including Oscar, I see now as people who understood that this business was always changing, and that today's easy money could go away tomorrow and so they were simply hyper-focused on making hay while the sun shined. Once I owned my own firm, this mindset became all too familiar a paradigm to me, and I became as "greedy" as anyone I once disparaged. I learned to embrace the realistic philosophy that anyone who says money isn't important never stood in a breadline.

At least DAG was honest about what motivated him, which I respected and even admired in a twisted sort of way. One morning I was standing next to him on the sidewalk outside the entrance to 30 South Wacker. He abruptly stooped over and reached for the ground; I thought he was tying his shoe. But he rose just as quickly and I noticed he had a dime in his hand. I looked at Oscar and smiled at the ludicrousness of a man with an eight-figure net worth in 1990 going out of his way to pick up a grime-caked dime accidentally dropped on a Chicago curb. He looked at me and flashed a wry grin. "Free money's free money."

I once asked Oscar why he never bothered to socialize with the other traders on the floor, other than the brokers who by necessity he was required to entertain. "I'm here to make money, not friends," he explained. He added sardonically: "If I want a friend I'll get a dog." And he was right. People came and went in the trading pits, much like those who sidle up to the craps table to lay down a marker or two, quickly crap out, and move on.

There were indeed some interesting characters, and I came to understand that the trading pit was in many ways the most honest place of business in which I have ever worked. Although perceived by the uninformed on the outside looking in as a den of privileged, if cutthroat, insider moneymen, the commodities trading floor was actually the great equalizer. Your pedigree, your MBA from Wharton, your summa cum laude from an Ivy League school meant nothing once you set foot on the floor. If you didn't have the uncanny, often innate and unteachable skill sets that made some great traders and others washouts, nothing else on your resume mattered. As the old cartoon showing a man sitting in a skid row alley in a rumpled business suit read: "Buy high, sell low, rode that idea right into the toilet!"

The various traders I got to know were pulled from a variety of backgrounds as diverse in experience as the USA itself. In my time there I stood next to a high school dropout tennis pro, a former Chicago Cubs pitcher, a Harvard Law grad, an old Hungarian immigrant who survived the Holocaust, a woman art historian, and a former Marine among others. The local flavor was still very much Chicago however, and pretty evenly split between the Chicagoland's ethnic factions of South Side Irish, West Side Italian, North Shore Jewish, and the WASP horse country to the northwest in Lake County. Though predominantly white, all races and ethnicities were represented; in this place the color that mattered most was green. Some were born-again Christians who made fortunes and then, having remained immune to the corrosive influences that surrounded them, went on to live their beliefs by setting up missions all over the world. Others became hopeless alcoholics or drug addicts. In such an environment, where one had to be sharp and energetic, cocaine use was common, as the locked doors of the floor bathroom stalls often testified. I saw more than my share of potential lives chewed up and spit out in the rock-star lifestyle that has been the plague of so many invincible young men suddenly flush with cash and free time. Whether a trader was an addict or teetotaler, angel or fiend, doctor or dock worker, a physicist or carpenter, white-collar dandy or blue-collar teamster, so many had what might be nicely labeled an *excess of personality* that soon I came to learn that when you're poor and crazy you're just "crazy." When you're rich and crazy, you're "eccentric."

Graduating from floor clerk to funded trader, "getting your badge," by no means guaranteed you'd make millions. I don't know the statistics, but my hunch is that for every successful floor trader I knew, ten either washed out completely or just never reached the financial heights as those who did have that intangible X factor. But for those lucky traders who did have the gift, so long as they kept their demons in check and showed up every day sharp and ready to trade, the sky was the limit. I got a sense of this when I once asked GATS if he had change for a hundred-dollar bill. He laid a paternal hand on my yellowcoat shoulder and smiled. "Little Shafe," he said, "that *is* change."

CHAPTER 7

PROMOTED

Several months into my new job, Oscar's trusted personal clerk was promoted to trader and shipped off to Southeast Asia to trade the Euroyen contract on the Singapore Mercantile Exchange (SMX). J. R. got his badge and would soon be trading currencies. So one morning Roselyn told me that my position from now on was to stand right behind Oscar, who by then was arguably the most powerful market-maker in the Eurodollar options pit. I was no longer an order taker, but rather positioned like a tandem skydiver glued to his back on the almighty top step and serving as the big boss's right-hand clerk. It was a promotion. And I knew my fraternal connection had nothing to do with this move up as it was just too important a position. This gave me a great sense of achievement; no doubt my brother breathed a sigh of relief as it was confirmation that he'd indeed brought Oscar a good hire in his younger sibling. My job was to stand behind this little moneymaking machine of a man and try to keep track of his many trades in real-time.

"Hey, Zack!" Oscar might suddenly yell as if zapped with a cattle prod. "Sell five hundred!" Then he'd fix his eyes on a broker across the pit. "Bets! Sold the Junes! Yes, balance sold! Sold!"

Then down to his lower left. "Barry! Baarrry! Goddammit, you asshole, buy the Seps! Eight hundred!"

"You're a sweet man, Oscar," the broker Barry would shout back while acknowledging the transaction and informing his clerk the client was filled.

Then Oscar would hand me three blank cards over his shoulder, turn his head slightly, and command me to "hedge 'em and card 'em up!"

I would then have to instantly reconstruct the series of trades in my head. My photographic memory came in handy here as in my mind's eye I watched the action I'd just observed in instant replay. I knew, for example, that Zack had been the one bidding .23 for the March 92.50 calls and Oscar just sold him 500. I carded that trade up (jotted the details down on one) and then, knowing that these calls had a .30 delta, for every 100 Oscar sold he would have to buy 30 March futures, so I motioned to one of the futures clerks, "March! Buy one-fifty!" (Five hundred times .30.) Next up I knew that Beatrice ("BETS") was the one bidding for 300 of the June 91.00 puts for .21 and Oscar had just sold her the "balance," which meant all BETS had left to buy; they had a delta of .18 and to hedge puts you do the same thing to the futures, not the opposite as in calls, so I flashed to the futures pit, "June sell fifty-four!" (300 times .18) and carded that one up. Then there was the September 93.25/94.50 call spread being offered by Barry "WULF" at .20 with a delta of .28, and Oscar bought 800, and 800 times .28 equals 224, so: "Hey! Sep sell two-twenty-four!" During the craziness Oscar would turn a 180 and grab me forcefully by the lapels until I'd almost fall backward off the step. With his nose practically touching mine he'd demand,

"Where are we?" I would quickly report to him the fills: "Um, you bought a hundred fifty Marches, sold fifty-four Junes, and sold two hundred twenty-four Seps. I'm confirming the prices now." His mind would race, whizzing through the calculations like a Turing engine, until he was satisfied that he was indeed properly hedged. Then he would turn back to face the seething mob and commence trading again.

The deep pockets in my yellow smock would fill with cards recording Oscar's many transactions in my handwriting, and then in the commotion I would feel a hand fish through them like a pickpocket and remove them. I'd look down to see one of the big-eyed young clerks grinning up at me, and I'd wink back as Oscar faced the pit hopping and weaving and screaming. Many were high school kids on summer break or college students taking a semester off; often as not they were siblings or cousins of traders, naturally. After emptying my pockets and before bringing them back to the input clerks stationed at PCs on the periphery of the exchange floor to type up and process the winners and losers into the various accounts, they'd make a motion to me that was thumb out, index finger up like an *L*, which meant, "Do you need a resupply of cards?" They were comparable to the drummer boys who passed out ammunition to the hotly engaged troops on the firing line. Sometimes they would also pass up to me the latest pricing sheets in rolled-up sheaves of paper, on which were printed-out spreadsheets showing complex financial models distilled into numbers and matrices, one for each month and every option stretching out several years. (Someone unfamiliar with options trading would no doubt read these sheets' contents with as much comprehension as an illiterate trying to decipher the Rosetta Stone.)

Sometimes there would be a sudden eruption of activity as an unexpected bit of news hit and the previously tranquil pits would explode in a frenzy of screaming and shoving and waving with apoplectic phone clerks on the horn with demanding traders from all over the world firing orders at them which they in turn were flashing at crazed arb clerks. The action could become so chaotic, with there being no real orderly bid-offer progressions but rather just prices flying about and trades hitting the tape willy-nilly, that the exchange reporters would get overwhelmed and simply couldn't report the last price that traded in an orderly fashion. This was what we called a "fast market," and though it may sound like slang it was an official term. In these frenetic trading explosions one could actually look up at the pricing boards which no longer displayed numbers but rather just read the word "FAST" across the board.

You can imagine that the pressures on arb clerks, especially those working for the big brokerage houses and receiving waves of orders flashed in from the ranks of phone clerks, could be paralyzing. There was this one kid who had a slight speech impediment, so we called him Simon in reference to Mike Myers's happy *SNL* British boy in the bathtub who did "draawrrings." (He was actually from Chicago's South Side and was Irish if anything.) Simon, who stood next to me when I was still positioned with J. R. between the futures and options pit, worked for one of the big brokerage houses, and during the mayhem of one such feeding frenzy he was losing it. It was clear he'd completely lost track of all the orders flashed into him and his eyes began to show that "thousand-yard stare" when men psychologically break under the relentless strain. He began gibbering nonsense like the Rain Man. "Five hundred gets a hundred gets a March with a carry the one three times filled ...," then into the Ralph Kramden "hamana hamana hamana" routine.

"The boy's speaking in tongues!" screamed J. R. over the commotion. "Hallelujah!" We all began chiding him mercilessly. "Can I get an amen!" I shouted. "Praise Jesus!" added another yellowcoat. "Hey Simon, I didn't know you was a snake handler!" said yet another.

Suddenly from one of the phone banks we could hear his assigned phone clerk's shrill voice pierce the noise and confusion. "*Simon*!" He was yelling, standing high up on his chair to be more visible with a phone to his ear. "Simon!" I shouted in the melee while grabbing him by the arm. "Look at your man there!" Simon turned and the red-faced phone clerk with the hot receiver to his ear flashed violently with his balled fist pushed off his forehead to sell a hundred-lot and then three fingers turned ninety degrees: "Sell One Hundred at Eight." This was the tipping point for the poor kid as that last bit of input completely short-circuited his overloaded motherboard. He suddenly began twirling in a circle like a ballerina while slamming his fist into his forehead and screaming wildly: "A fist at eight! A fist at eight! A fist at eight!"

His filling broker facing the futures pit looked over his shoulder. "Fan-fucking-tastic! The kid's lost it! What the fuck are you saying, Simon?!"

"A fist at eight!" he kept screaming in a panic. "A fist at eight!"

"Get him the hell out of here!" the furious broker screamed. "Anyone know what this Mary's jabbering about?"

I leaned in to the broker and directed his attention toward the irate phone clerk. "I think he wants you to sell a hundred at eight, but you better make sure with him."

The broker nodded in thanks and managed to get the order executed for the relieved phone clerk who had a Limey from a London bank on the other side of the pond angrily demanding to know: "Am I bloody filled at eight or not, mate?"

Simon left the floor and was never seen again.

Day in and day out, week after week, the markets rose and fell or just stayed stagnant. The intensity of the day and the bodily exertion required took its physical toll on me. "Rough and tumble" sometimes had literal connotations. My back would often burn and ache. And the noise was at times so ear-splitting that within a year I'd developed the first symptoms of tinnitus. No doubt the metallic buzzing I still hear when all is quiet stems from numerous incidents of traders literally shouting at the tops of their lungs one inch away from and directly into my ear. I liked the trading floor and got off on the vibe, but I couldn't see myself doing this when I was forty. But that was a long way off. At the moment I considered my time as Oscar's clerk to be a kind of paid grad school. I learned more about business and options trading in particular than I ever could have from a classroom. Oscar said I was acquiring knowledge through "osmosis." What struck me was the velocity of money and how quickly vast sums could be made and lost in the time it takes to order a burger and fries at the drive-through. Louis Winthorpe in the movie *Trading Places* wasn't kidding when offering Billy Ray Valentine his pep talk before stepping into the fictional Frozen Concentrated Orange Juice pit:

"Nothing you have ever experienced will prepare you for the absolute carnage you're about to witness. Super Bowl? World Series? They don't know what pressure is. In this building it's either kill or be killed. You make no friends in the pits and you take no prisoners. One minute you're up a half million in soybeans and the next, boom! Your kids don't go to college and they've repossessed your Bentley."

I mention *Trading Places* several times in this story for a couple of reasons. First off, that film was to floor traders what *Caddyshack* was to golfers or *This Is Spinal Tap* to rock musicians: a common cultural reference for a cadre of different personalities, backgrounds, and educations all brought together by an exclusively unique and shared experience only those on the inside truly comprehended. "The Duke brothers are buying" was a generic explanation for market activity not easily explained away, and at the end of the trading day one would invariably shout Don Ameche's frantic demand to "Turn those machines back on!"

The second reason I bring up the film is that it was my first inclination that there were actually commodities trading pits in New York. I'd always associated New York with stocks and bonds and Chicago with their redheaded stepchild, commodities. But in fact, there were full-on exchanges there with their own floors: the Commodities Exchange (COMEX), where they traded gold and precious metals; the Coffee, Sugar and Cocoa Exchange, which was self-explanatory; and, most relevant to my future, the New York Mercantile Exchange (NYMEX). And much to my surprise, in the summer of 1990 Oscar asked me to relocate there and clerk for his trader who'd just set up the FGT New York office and was trading on the NYMEX. Having spent all of my formative years in Illinois, I was game for an adventure. The position would be temporary, and I'd really be helping Oscar out as he wanted a good clerk to help make sure his latest venture was launched on a solid foundation. I'd get a nice raise and they'd pay for my hotel room until I found an apartment. Best of all, upon my return I would be rewarded with a coveted trading badge and my career would be in full swing. How could I say no?

"Sure," I said. "I'll do it." Oscar thanked me. "What do they trade on the NYMEX?" I asked.

Oscar said: "Crude oil."

Three weeks later I was in Manhattan.

CHAPTER 8

IF I CAN MAKE IT THERE...

I GREW UP THINKING CHICAGO was "the big city," and with a population in 1990 of 2.8 million it was nothing to shrug off. But when my flight landed at LaGuardia and the weathered checkered taxi whisked me across the Queensboro Bridge over the East River into Manhattan, I soaked in the sprawling, towering immensity of New York City with mouth agape. For the first time in my life I found myself feeling quite insignificant. As the filthy cab jostled me across the island through Midtown toward the Theater District and my waiting hotel, I marveled at the many tall buildings reaching up to a sepia sky jammed up one against another to line the wide avenues forming great canyon walls of marble, stone, and glass. Each edifice would have been a standout skyscraper in downtown Chicago. But here they just blended one into the next in a scope and scale I had never before imagined.

The fact is Gotham intimidated the hell out of me. I'd been comfortable in the pits of Chicago...everyone knew me, and I knew them. Plus, my University of Illinois background and suburban Chicago upbringing, not to mention having family working thirty feet away from me, gave me a sense of pedigree on the CME. I often ran into pit acquaintances and fellow Illini alums at the Chicago Health Club after work or in the bars and even just out on the streets in the evening. The Windy City felt more to me like a very large small town. That prenatal existence was all gone now. To reference John Adams, I'd taken a leap into the dark.

I settled into my temporary home, one of the 1,331 rooms in the twenty-seven-floor Milford Plaza hotel on the corner of Eighth Avenue and Forty-Fourth Street, just two blocks from the hustle and bustle of Times Square. Today that area has been gentrified and disinfected and made safe for families and traveling nuns. Street caricaturists, live bands, food vendors, and activists line the sidewalks, while mini-entrepreneurs manning little carts ply their wares in a parklike setting that was once a busy intersection but now is a cordoned-off pedestrian thoroughfare. Sweaty would-be actors dressed as colorful Disney characters stroll the open square waving and obliging giddy tourists by posing for random photographs before they grab a bite at Europa Cafe or shop in Skagen Denmark. But back when I first arrived it was a filthy, seedy part of town. This was before Rudy Giuliani put an end to the mayhem run amok in a world-class city that was so fraught with crime and decay and X-rated movie theaters and drug pushers and prostitutes that the movie *The Warriors* didn't seem so much like cult fiction as a legitimate reflection of daily life. I'd gone from the leafy womb of suburban Illinois to the dystopia of Midtown Manhattan. Culture shock, anyone?

And yet, something about the old cheer "If I can make it there, I'll make it anywhere!" rang true to me, and I vowed to rise above my fears and unexpected sudden loneliness to the challenge. What choice did I have anyway? I had a job to do.

• • •

The next morning I made my dazed and confused way over to the Forty-Second Street Port Authority MTA station and bus terminal and descended into the intestinal tract of the Manhattan subway system. It seemed that a small colony of unwashed and mentally deranged homeless people called the Port Authority home and the subterranean world reeked of urine and city grime and acrid electric fumes. I hopped on what I hoped was the southbound E train and zoomed downtown to the World Trade Center. Popping up somewhere around Cortland Street I then trekked farther down the lower tip of the island into a completely different world. The energy of money here, just blocks from the New York Stock Exchange, amidst the stone and steel facades of lofty skyscrapers and busy plazas that now stood where once was the north side of the protective wall that gave its name to the famous street of the original Dutch settlement of New Amsterdam, was palpable. If Chicago was the center of one part of the US economy, New York's financial district was the center of that economy itself, indeed the world's.

After a disoriented search I found the First Global satellite office. It was just a dingy room on the fifth floor of an ancient building on Liberty Street across from the commodities exchange floor, which was housed within the low-rise black-girded 4 World Trade Center. There I met the first and only employee who manned Oscar's newest outpost on the financial frontier.

Alan, the man running the little office, had just turned thirty. He carried himself with much more maturity and poise than I. The two of us would have to see to all of the responsibilities usually carried out by several staff in the main Chicago office. I would soon find myself learning from Alan how to be not just a clerk, but a manager of sorts. It was yet another bit of education courtesy of my "paid grad school." I learned that while I was very good at mastering the concepts and execution skills behind trading complex derivatives—which is what futures and options are—my more mundane clerical skills needed work. In Chicago I could lean on the other clerks to run the trading sheets, have cards at the ready, or make sure the latest positions were inputted correctly into the system from which Oscar would derive his risk and P&L. Alan, by contrast, was a details man...the type who double-dotted his *i* and double-crossed his *t*. He was most likely someone who watched Phil Hartman's SNL character "The Anal-Retentive Chef" and found it odd that others were laughing. One might say that for Alan spontaneity had its time and place.

After the awkward first meeting with my new boss, I took stock of my new office away from the floor. Unlike the modern twin towers of 10 and 30 South Wacker, this building was ancient and rundown. The dark hardwood floor had a century of scuffs, it was obvious nothing more than a ceremonial mop had ever been splatted over its surface, and the paint covering the steam radiators (yes, steam radiators) was chipped. They probably hadn't been painted since the Johnson administration. The windows, however, had been painted so many times they were sealed shut. It was tough to see through the greasy filth coating the glass. Given the noise and pollution outside, what would have been the point of opening a window, anyway? So, FGT New York was one room, two windows, one dot-matrix printer, one laptop, one TV, one transplanted clerk, and one trader.

I was not thrilled to be there. And yet, my disappointment in the Dickensian office was but a prelude to the dismay I would feel upon entering the old NYMEX floor itself. With our one clunky (and quite heavy) Toshiba laptop and trading sheets in hand, I followed my new boss across Liberty Street to 4 World Trade Center. Alan was one of those speed-walker types whose unreasonably rapid gait compelled me to follow him almost at a trot. It gave me a more subordinate appearance, as I felt like a young assistant following a diva around backstage with a toy poodle cradled in one arm and a latte splashing all over my sleeve in the other. Oscar always treated me with respect. Yes, he signed my paychecks, and no doubt he was *the man*. But he also appreciated that his clerks hustled and worked long hours for low wages, all with one purpose: to make him filthy rich. Alan seemed to feel I was just an underling. Maybe his Cornell to my U of I had something to do with it. The Northeast as a whole, I would discover, cared far more for academic pedigree, and with few exceptions the closer to one of the two coasts the school, the more prestige one's degree was granted. Although, as with Chicago, the commodities trading pits here bucked that elitist mindset.

"The pits" was an apt moniker for the trading floor. I got my photo ID from security and made my way up the escalator to the seventh floor where one arrived at the three-story-high exchange, which carved out the center of levels seven, eight, and nine. Approaching the entrance, I could hear the familiar roar of dealing, and my heart started to race with excitement. But as I stepped onto the trading arena that same heart sank, and an acute pang of remorse and the idea that perhaps I'd made a terrible mistake hit me.

The floor was, quite simply, a dump. In every way it fell short of the high-flying, modern CME, from the infrastructure to the physical appearance, to even the tired look of the people who populated the poorly lit, dreary, and drab space. The first thing I noticed was that I wasn't standing on hard rubber flooring that so aided traction when being jostled about on the CME but instead found myself looking down at a filthy and weathered ruby-red carpet. One can only imagine the condition of such a rug after years of use and abuse under the shuffling feet of a mob of traders and their clerks tracking in everything their sneakers sopped up off the trash-laden streets of Manhattan. The color was now more of a grim sienna than the original bright red. It was also torn in many places and crudely repaired with hasty applications of silver duct tape.

The phone booths lining the rings, as they called the trading pits, were of slapdash construction, cramped, and as about as well maintained as the carpet. And the phones themselves were of the same model one might find hanging on a Levittown kitchen wall in 1975. At least they weren't rotary, which was a small technological triumph. The pits themselves were considerably smaller than the massive Chicago Eurodollar or bond pits, and thus could three distinct exchanges share one large open space. I found it odd that you could easily move from one floor to the other with no barriers. The only way you really could tell that you'd crossed from the NYMEX into the COMEX or the Coffee, Sugar and Cocoa was that the badges changed in color from lemon yellow to deep orange to forest green, respectively.

The NYMEX officials were positioned about the crowd like referees. They sported yellow coats not unlike CME clerks. (This took me a little time to get used to.) The rules of the exchange were such that only the seller in any trade was responsible for carding it up. White cards for futures, blue for options. But unlike Chicago, wherein you held onto them until a clerk came by to collect them, these cards were given directly to the exchange input clerks to record. To me, the most curious sights of this new exchange were the inputters positioned down at the very bottom and dead center of each ring. They stood like hubs encircled by a spastic wheel of colors. Odder still, they were enveloped in waist-high fish netting. They wore goggles, which I thought strange…until I realized why. After they wrote up a trade, the sellers didn't hand over the cards so much as wrist-flick them at the reporters who either caught them in midair or felt them ricochet off their bodies to be fished out of the netting. They would furiously input the trades into machines while trying to stay ahead of the volleys of cardboard projectiles raining down on them. Some traders purposely tried to hit the reporters in the heads, like target practice. A few even got to be skilled marksmen. This was why the inputters wore eye protection. In busy times the air would be filled with cards spinning and twirling like frisbees sailing into the center of the ring as if caught in a gravitational vortex. But the eyewear could not shield the hard-working reporters from the sprays of spittle that traders on all sides screaming at the top of their lungs routinely showered down on them. I found it all somewhat demeaning. But, as with the Chicago pits and their own peculiarities, the system worked.

The traders themselves appeared to me a grittier, more street-hewn lot than the Chicago crew. Several of them didn't even wear trading jackets at all but clipped their yellow NYMEX badges (two-inch-by-four-inch rectangles rather than Chicago's larger squares) right onto the chests of their collared shirts. Many were from Brooklyn, Staten Island, the Bronx, or the coastal New Jersey area. They tended to have voices like the Little Rascal Froggy in the *Our Gang* shorts, as if their shredded vocal cords lacked the elasticity of those crooners in Chicago. The gruff shouts combined with a propensity to pronounce "th" as "d" and ignore the letter *R* altogether gave these rough, stocky, often unshaven men the aura of dockyard workers rather than purveyors of products of high finance. A few were from more affluent surroundings in Long Island or Westchester, but for the most part this exchange was a blue-collar haven with a lot of guys whose last names ended in vowels. The Ivy League prepsters were at the New York Stock Exchange down the block, some of whom still sported bowties and Roman numerals in their names, or in one of the surrounding high-rises ensconced at investment banks or hedge funds.

But in the summer of 1990, these traders who chugged along somewhat under the radar at the NYMEX—which in the years before it became the hub of pricing for the most important raw material on the planet was a potato exchange—would suddenly find themselves in the economic vortex of a global crisis that would make and destroy many fortunes and careers in the months ahead.

In that same summer, Oscar's Sauron-like eye for opportunity had turned eastward and sensed there were profits to be mined in the energy pits. It was his business acumen that prompted the hiring of Alan and sending out a senior clerk to help launch FGT New York. It was an expansion conceived and executed with the remarkable efficiency and speed only a trader of supreme confidence, deep pockets, and appetite for risk like Oscar could pull off. It was as if he had a sixth sense for opportunity...what the Germans call *Fingerspitzengefühl*, or literally "intuition at the fingertips."

But not even Oscar with all his prescience could have foreseen what was to come.

• • •

As I was learning how to deal with this new and rather grim workplace, halfway around the world along the sweltering shores of the Persian Gulf, war clouds were brewing. And in 1990 there was nothing better for crude oil traders than a good old-fashioned Middle East war. And thanks to a sadistic madman with delusions of grandeur in Baghdad and a no-nonsense former World War II Navy pilot in Washington, DC, that's exactly what they got.

CHAPTER 9

"REGRETTABLY"

On August 2, 1990, Saddam Hussein, the bloodthirsty dictator of the Republic of Iraq, sent his planes, tanks, and infantry across an invisible surveyor's line that ran along a wasteland of desert, roughly where the Mediterranean Levant ends and the Arabian Peninsula begins, smashing into the tiny country of Kuwait. While Iraq officially claimed Kuwait was stealing its oil via slant drilling, its true motives were more complicated and less clear. At the time of the invasion, Iraq owed Kuwait $14 billion in outstanding debt, which the wealthy emirate had loaned Saddam's regime during his nasty 1980–1988 war with Iran. In addition, Iraq felt Kuwait was overproducing oil, lowering prices, and hurting Iraqi export profits in a time of financial stress.

Prior to the invasion, Iraq and Kuwait had been producing a combined 4.3 million barrels of oil a day. This loss of flow, coupled with threats to Saudi Arabia's additional daily production of 6 million barrels, which was roughly 25 percent of OPEC's total output, led to a sudden rise in prompt month oil futures prices from $21 per barrel at the end of July to $28 per barrel on August 6. This was the day when the United Nations Security Council followed up a call for Iraq to leave Kuwait with a worldwide ban on trade with Saddam's regime. It also banned the importation of oil from either Iraq or Kuwait, effectively choking off 7 percent of the daily supply of crude to a world that voraciously consumed roughly 64 million barrels per day. (In response to this ban Saddam formally annexed Kuwait on August 8.) Alarmed by the threat to the stability of the most oil-rich region on the planet, and as a matter of principle, President George H. W. Bush made it known in no uncertain terms that Saddam's invasion was viewed by the White House as a flagrant act of aggression that "will not stand." If the Iraqi military did not voluntarily leave Kuwait, it would be expelled by force. As the United Nations, led by the United States and NATO, built up a military presence in the region, and Saddam's own Kuwaiti occupying force swelled to three hundred thousand troops, oil prices steadily climbed to a peak of $46 per barrel in mid-October.

While stories of mayhem and murder and plunder dribbled out of the imprisoned Kuwait, a looming question remained: in the face of the awesome firepower of the international coalition arraying against him, would Saddam blink and hightail it back into Iraq? Or would the US and its United Nations allies have to blast him out? No one knew. But such uncertainty over there in the sands of Arabia meant a license to print money for the giddy NYMEX traders over here at 4 World Trade Center. And the longer the tensions dragged on the more money these traders would make.

Trading is not the same thing as investing. An investor in the stock of a concern like Apple is betting that the company will keep on growing in value and thus buys a share in the company. The company then uses the proceeds to build and expand and in turn make each share that much more valuable. In the end, an IPO is one way of raising investor capital. With the exceptions of a few rogue short-sellers, it's in everyone's common interest for equities to go up. When the numbers are green an investor has a "good" day. When red, not so much.

But trading futures on raw materials, which is what commodities are, is not an intrinsically bullish operation. Commodities' prices fluctuate depending on supply and demand. Prices go up and they go down with indifference. And since a futures contract is an agreement to buy or sell a certain standardized amount of a commodity (in oil's case each futures contract equals a thousand barrels) at a specific price at a predetermined time in the future, one can effectively go "long" or "short" with equal dexterity and thus profit from both a rise (long) or a fall (short) in prices. Later on, when I briefly became an oil trader myself at Texaco, I used to come home from work and a cheery neighbor would say to me innocently: "Hey, I see oil was up. You must have had a good day, huh?" I'd flash a tired smile and politely explain to him that I was, in fact, short oil and thus had a bad day. "How can ya sell somethin' ya don't own?" he'd ask, scratching his head quizzically.

So, as I learned the ropes of a new exchange (while also landing an apartment in Hoboken, New Jersey, so I could vacate my room at the Milford Plaza, which was starting to feel like a prison cell) oil trading reached a fever pitch on the NYMEX floor. Every day from August into the fall through to Thanksgiving and Christmas traders voraciously gobbled up profits in the heavy volume and extreme volatility of the whipsawing crude oil futures and options markets driven by hair-trigger uncertainties that would suddenly lurch prices this way and that. So crazy was the wheeling and dealing that I would often find myself checking Alan's trading records, which dealers jotted on long notepads along with the trading cards for the exchange, wherein on the left side was a buy of 200 for 41.20 and on the right a nearly simultaneous notation of a sale of 200 at 41.25. At $10.00 per penny, this is a quick turnaround of $10,000 (1,000 barrels times 200 times .05). In less time than it took me to pen these words. Alan always insisted on writing up his own tickets, naturally. That was fine with me. One less way for me to screw up. And on this floor at this time one mistake could have devastating consequences given the market's whiplash-inducing volatility.

On November 29, 1990, the UN Security Council officially authorized the use of force against Iraq if it did not voluntarily evacuate Kuwait by January 15, 1991. The war clouds were growing ever more dark and ominous. This was just more good news for the oil pit as uncertainty not only begets pricing inefficiencies but heavy volume, allowing one to simultaneously buy low and sell high large blocks with little exposure. The world was taking no chances, and they were buying or selling futures as needed at a frantic pace to mitigate risk. And what could be riskier than being dependent upon a commodity wherein much of it at the time was produced right smack-dab in the middle of a potential Armageddon? Not only was the flow of oil from Iraq and Kuwait suddenly off the market, but Saddam's misadventure had the potential to ignite a regional conflagration by threatening Saudi Arabia's daily output while tempting the fanatical theocracy of Iran (Saddam's arch enemy) to choke off the Strait of Hormuz, through which 20 percent of all crude oil exports passed. It was a global crisis of literally biblical proportions as Saddam vowed to launch missiles at tiny Israel should the United Nations try to expel him from Kuwait by force of arms. His hope was to prompt the hated Jewish state to retaliate in self-defense and turn the oil conflict into an Arab-versus-West internecine showdown that would shatter the fragile alliance confronting him...one that included military contributions from Egypt, Saudi Arabia, Syria, the UAE, Oman, and Qatar. High-stakes poker indeed.

The stakes were high on the NYMEX floor as well. This was new territory so prices continued to fluctuate wildly amidst the fog of confusion as to what this all meant at the end of the day to crude supplies. Did the Friday, September 14 British and French announcements of their deployment of troops to the region increase the odds that Iraq would flinch and peace (and the flow of oil) be assured? *Sell!* Or...maybe it meant the battle would be just that much bigger, bloodier, and more destructive once the shit hit the fan. *Buy!* Sell! Buy! Mine! Yours! Buy 100 for 31.02! Sell you 100 at 31.07! Card it up! Five Gs in five seconds. *Ka-ching! Ka-ching!* As word of the ungodly sums of money being printed in crude oil spread across the exchange and onto The Street itself, the number of new traders who suddenly appeared in the mosh pit swelled an estimated four-fold. The crowd overflowed to the point where it was not uncommon for a trader to be squeezed out and shot from the ring as if popped from a pimple and come careening down onto his back into the aisle as you walked by.

The waterfall of profits was so steady that every moment spent off the floor, whether to grab lunch or even just use the toilet, could cost thousands in lost opportunities. So vital was trading time that some firms went to extraordinary lengths to make sure their people were in position and raring to go when the opening buzzer sounded. One firm even went so far as to pick up their star trader every Monday morning and whisk him by helicopter from his Long Island home to lower Manhattan just to make sure no traffic jams from returning Hamptons revelers delayed his commute. It was money well spent.

Meanwhile, Saddam himself was spewing forth defiant statements on a daily basis. They instantly made their way onto the analog electronic news ticker hovering above our heads.

> -- Saddam – "We are not intimidated by the size of the armies or the type of hardware the US has brought." -- [November 12]

Or...

> --Saddam – "Allah is on our side. That is why we will beat the aggressor." -- [December 12]

And so on, and so forth. The dictator's bellicose proclamations only served to toss lighter fluid on the bonfire of uncertainty...and by unintended consequence shower cash like confetti onto the NYMEX floor. One trader leaned over to me: "I fuckin' *love* dis guy!"

Such was the global crisis in the second half of 1990. What was a looming disaster for the world was manna from Heaven for the NYMEX oil traders who would eventually earn the envied sobriquets of "Gulf War babies" as this was the time in which their fortunes were made. After the hectic trading session was over and the day's profits tallied up—which translated into stacks of money higher than anyone on this sleepy backwater exchange could have dreamt of just a year before—many would retire to Suspenders pub on Greenwich Street and strain bottle upon bottle through already overworked livers (these guys didn't look very good for all their riches). They would drink and carouse and backslap the night away, all the while pondering what "So Damned Insane," as Alan called Saddam Hussein, would do next. "I don't know what he's got up his sleeve," I once heard a drunken dealer for Drexel say while lining up shots. "But I sure as shit hope he takes his own sweet time doin' it."

• • •

But, in the end, it really wasn't up to Saddam. For all his bluster, he'd bitten off more than he could chew and as the weeks went by he found himself facing an ever-growing United Nations force that would eventually number somewhere north of 700,000 ground troops supported by over four thousand warplanes, thirty-two hundred tanks, and two hundred ships (including six US aircraft carriers and an unspecified number of nuclear submarines). An admirably united world saw Saddam's army currently laying waste to his tiny neighbor as an abscess that had to be lanced. Soon the time would come to launch what Saddam promised in a misplaced bravura flourish would be "the mother of all battles." To be sure, the Muslim nations—and even Europe—had no love for the United States or President Bush, who'd skillfully cobbled together this ubercoalition. But they loathed the idea of Saddam Hussein controlling the region's oil even more. So they went along.

Still, there was one last chance to settle this whole mess peacefully and avoid war with all the grisly aftermath, from the heavy loss of life to oil price shocks, it surely promised.

Everything came to a head one week before the UN deadline for Iraqi forces to get the hell out of Dodge expired. On January 9, 1991, US Secretary of State James Baker III and Iraqi foreign minister Tariq Aziz met in Geneva behind closed doors in an eleventh-hour attempt to avoid violence. This meeting, which would last for six hours, began at 11:00 a.m. local time, which was 5:00 a.m. in New York. As the traders filed in to take up their usual positions that morning an eerie quiet hung over the exchange. There's a scene in *Trading Places* in the mythical Orange Juice pit[3] where the traders all stop what they're doing and gather around the TV screen at the center of the ring. They stand in silence, anxiously awaiting the agriculture secretary's reading of the confidential crop reports. It was something like that for real when the Geneva summit concluded at roughly 11:00 a.m. EST and word hit that Secretary Baker was about to make a statement. But instead of an actual television set we craned our necks up to the electronic news ticker board that scrolled a steady stream of market news and quotes above us. This would tell the men and women who traded the very commodity most impacted by his looming announcement whether the path Saddam had chosen was peace or war. The exchange floor was so subdued that even the most hushed conversations were clearly audible above the low ambient sounds. All eyes were on the news board. Then the first words began their horizontal right-to-left crawl.

-- Baker -- "Regrettably...in over six hours of talks...I heard nothing today that suggested to me

---

3   The scene featuring the non-existent FCOJ pit was actually filmed in the gold futures pit on the COMEX.

any Iraqi flexibility whatsoever on complying with
the United Nations Security Council Resolution" --

All anyone on the floor needed to see was "Regrettably...."
There it was. No one even bothered to read the rest. One gruff
older broker with a sense of nostalgia shouted: "It's war, I tell ya!
War!" Immediately the exchange exploded in earsplitting pan-
demonium as futures prices surged higher. "Watch your heads,
boys! They love the crude!" screamed one exuberant trader
who'd come in long and was now being handsomely compen-
sated for his risk-taking. I did a double take when I looked over
to the crude oil futures pit and saw two ebullient traders, who
were obviously long, slam into each other in an elated bear
hug. One was my size at around 180 pounds and the other a
burly fellow north of 250, and the 70-pound weight difference
caused them to lose their balance and tumble off the steps to
land on the ancient red carpet with a dull thud. They continued
to roll around on the filthy rug in the valley between the crude
oil and heating oil rings backslapping like two men engaged in
a sloppy bar brawl. I found myself unable to resist grinning as
I took in the moment of the NYMEX's greatest triumph, even
though this meant little financial windfall for me as I was still
just a clerk. No doubt it meant free drinks at Suspenders later
so that was something.

As he traded furiously, Alan had an oddly subdued look
on his face. He was well aware of the torrent of gold pouring
into his and other dealers' coffers in the frenzied trading cas-
cading back and forth as institutional buyers and sellers from
all over the world came into the pits and crossed absurdly wide
bid-offers to get their orders filled. Alan dutifully took advan-

tage of the chaos as would a man in one of those glass booths with dollar bills whirring around him who tries to grab as many as he can and stuff them into his pockets before the machine turns off...but he was a mature and decent guy who was able to look past his P&L to contemplate what the advent of war meant. As for most of us, it really didn't cross our minds what Baker's words portended for the young men and women in uniform half a world away. While traders high-fived and counted their winnings, in the sands of Arabia hundreds of thousands of troops were cleaning their rifles, arming their tanks, fueling their warplanes, and waiting with trepidation for their orders... orders that would call on them to risk their lives to liberate a tiny emirate that cared little for them but whose country sat atop a lake of black gold the West simply couldn't live without and was willing to shed its children's blood to keep flowing.

• • •

One crazy, exhausting, profitable week later, at 2:58 a.m. local time on January 17, 1991, Operation Desert Shield, as the pre-war build-up was called, became Operation Desert Storm. It was dinner time in New York as we along with the rest of the world tuned in to the broadcasts from the upstart Cable News Network's Baghdad-embedded reporters and were treated to images beamed in real-time showing incoming missiles slamming into Iraq's capital city, and indeed across the entire war zone from Saddam's aerodromes to the trenches housing his cowering army and exposed armor. (In a callous demonstration of utter detachment given that I come from a family whose patriarch was wounded in the Korean War, I actually watched the opening salvos that meant terrified people were starting to die violent, painful deaths from the comfort of a hot tub.)

The initial aerial bombardment came courtesy of stealth bombers roaming the Iraqi skies at will laying well-placed ordnance with pinpoint accuracy onto targets unhidden by the cloak of night in this modern high-tech "Nintendo war"; high explosives knifed in from the sea as waves of Tomahawk missiles launched from warships cruising well out in the Persian Gulf screamed over the moonlit desert at treetop level; the attack came in the form of conventional fourth-generation fighter-bombers like carrier-based FA-18 Hornets and land-based F-16 Falcons or British Tornados that lit up the night sky as their bombs and rockets found their marks, and explosions and fireballs curled high into the humid air along the swamps of the Tigris and Euphrates Rivers. Each detonation announced to Saddam and his inept generals that the full weight of an American-led aerial offensive not seen since Operation Linebacker II in Vietnam had been unleashed upon them. "Cry 'Havoc,' and let slip the dogs of war!"

Those traders who went home long crude oil that night were surely ecstatic as they watched the battle they'd hoped for commence literally before their very eyes in a live fashion that our parents watching days-old footage from Vietnam, the first "living room war," never imagined. Pre-war analysis concluded that a war could cause oil prices to spike to $60.00 in the near term. Thus, did the longs pop champagne into the night as they expected to make a hefty profit come tomorrow's opening bell. Certainly a shooting war on the very ground that sat above some of the largest proven crude reserves on the planet was bullish for oil futures. Wasn't it?

Not necessarily.

Throughout the evening, as the relentless bombardment continued, uncontested by Iraq's overwhelmed defenses, over at the Pentagon briefing room, US defense secretary Dick Cheney and Joint Chiefs commander General Colin Powell briefed the press and fielded questions. Each answer they gave could have a major impact on how oil prices would behave tomorrow. I think I can pinpoint the exact moment when the longs started to get a little nervous. "We are not prepared to release any specifics now," said Cheney, "but I will simply say that the preliminary reports we have received in terms of the success of the operation, and that includes the possibility of casualties, have been very, very encouraging." This was as close as the taciturn Cheney could ever bring himself to throwing a high-five. What became clear to anyone watching the first phase of the war unfold was that the Iraqi armed forces were hopelessly outclassed, outmanned, outgunned, and outgeneraled. All across the war zone Saddam's conscripts were being decimated by aerial hellfire, which was intended to induce a catchphrase born of a later Iraq war but applicable here as well called "shock and awe." Saddam had gambled and lost big time. It became obvious within hours that what he promised would be "the mother of all battles" was setting up to be the mother of all routs. The technological disparity between the hyper-advanced US military and its allies and the primitive Iraqis was beyond overwhelming.

For oil markets craving some sense of direction to quell the uncertainty and drain the air from the volatility bubble, Cheney and Powell provided clarity. Whatever was to come in the fight ahead, it would be quick, if violent, and totally one-sided. Kuwait would very soon be rid of the uninvited guests camped within its borders. From a trader's perspective, this was an extremely bearish development.

By the time we walked onto the NYMEX floor the next morning, blurry-eyed from staying up most of the night to follow the unfolding victory, the opening call was *ten dollars lower.* For those who went home very long the night before and had their prayers for a shooting war answered, a financial disaster awaited them in the morning.

• • •

At the end of the trading day immediately following the opening of hostilities, crude futures closed at $21.44, having plunged $10.56. This was an unprecedented 33 percent collapse in price. In fact, this level actually represented a dime lower than where oil had been trading on August 1, 1990, the day before Saddam invaded. As one energy executive and former colleague told the *Wall Street Journal* that day: "If you said to any trader that we're going to have a war tonight and tomorrow the market will be down [ten] dollars-per-barrel they'd look at you as if you were a lunatic." But the lunacy had become a reality, and for every futures contract a bullish trader went home long that night he found his account depleted by $10,000.

This was precisely why Oscar vehemently forbade his traders from taking speculative positions. We were traders, he would remind us, market-makers, not investors. I once asked him the ol' "Whaddya think here, Oscar, up or down?" and he gave me a curt reply: "All I care about is what's the bid and what's the offer. You got that?" I got it. He didn't need to pay for a seat lease to sit upstairs and speculatively punt long or short. If possible, he always went home "flat," which meant having neither a bullish nor bearish position. It was a view that Alan, who over the course of the fourth quarter 1990 and first quarter 1991 made Oscar a small fortune from his initial foray into the Big Apple, fully shared. Even if you have a crystal ball that can tell you exactly what events will take place in the world tomorrow you just never know how the markets will collectively digest the news. As he said, Oscar was all about buying on the bid and selling on the offer. And waking up refreshed and unaffected by overnight market activity, ready for the trading opportunities that awaited him every day... even more so this day for his man in the crude oil pits during a shooting war in the Persian Gulf.

As the daily obliteration from the air rained down on Saddam's hapless armed forces, oil continued to gyrate, albeit at a much lower handle. But perceived options volatility as reflected in the premiums being charged by sellers, which can be distilled down to a financial expression of how much anxiety is in the market, was way down. One way to illustrate the concept is this typical scenario. If on the day before war began, with oil trading at $31, you may have thought to yourself: *hmmm, I bet war is imminent and if this happens, we're sure to go to $45, $50, maybe higher, even.* After all, war would disrupt supply flow, leading to an oil shortage. If the current price is $31.00 per barrel, you may be willing to buy a bunch of $40 call options to profit should the price of oil futures indeed surge higher when the shooting starts. Anyone selling these options has unlimited risk in a major rally. At the moment the $40 calls are nine full dollars out-of-the-money, and if they expired today, they would have no value. They'd be worth zero as no one is going to pay for the right to buy anything for nine bucks more than it currently is trading…unless there's time for this to change. That's why you're willing to pay a hefty premium for your $40 calls. They may soon be worth a lot in wartime. Sellers of the option know that all they can make is what the buyer pays them. But their losses could be enormous if oil goes from $31 to $50 to $60-plus and suddenly they have to sell oil $10, even $20 below value (a far greater loss than any cash they take in on the initial sale). And so, they will exact a very steep premium to sell something that, though seemingly worthless at this moment, has the potential given the uncertainty to become quite valuable. Thus, the steeper price the sellers demand is a measure of anxiety and uncertainty regarding future volatility. In the vernacular of trading, volatility (or simply "vol") is "bid."

What happens then if the war looks like it'll be quick work, no oil supply lines will be disrupted, and fears of future stock depletion are unfounded? Your calls would collapse in value. The possibility of the price climbing above $40 has evaporated, and now you own all these $40 calls that have very little if any chance of ever amounting to anything. Therefore, you'll want to sell them out quickly, as they will most likely expire worthless. But now no one will pay any premium for a right to buy crude for $40 when the odds of it getting there are remote at best given the severe pasting Saddam's boys are receiving in the field. So, the value of these call options collapses as badly as the underlying price of oil itself. The curtain hiding the unknown future has now been pulled back. With the real impact—or rather nonimpact—of the war now clear to the market, the uncertainty, the driver of options value or "vol," and really in essence what options traders buy and sell, has evaporated.

This "volatility implosion" laid waste to some bullish options dealers just as badly as the collapse of the price of oil itself decimated futures traders' accounts. They went home long not just in the direction of the price of oil itself but also owned many options whose value had become overly inflated in the uncertainty leading up to the opening shots of what ended up being a desert turkey shoot for the UN coalition. Now the verdict was in. Personal fortunes were obliterated.

As I walked onto the trading floor that first day after the war started I could gauge just by the looks on traders' faces who'd gone home "long and wrong" and who hadn't. Needless to say, a few of the guys with haggard, pale looks rarely appeared on the floor over the course of the week. Often another trader or broker from maybe another pit who worked for the miss-ing man's clearing firm—or futures commission merchant (FCM)—where the besieged accounts were housed would make an appearance and commence a flurry of trades with odd sizes like selling 678 of this call or 392 of that put, giving away enormous value to the lucky ones like Alan who knew better than to bet entire trading stakes on there being rationality in the Middle East. They were clearly unloading the vanished trader's positions in a fire sale to close out what remained of his once seven-, even eight-figure account.

The executioner would say blandly: "Okay, how are Novy thirty-three calls?" The traders would all be waiting bright-eyed, like goldfish hovering just beneath the surface while a generous child stands over them preparing to drop flecks of his hot dog bun into the water. They knew there would be a lot of liquida-tions, so they all agreed to keep the markets nice and wide, and thus transact at more profitable prices. If an option was valued at .25, instead of making the bid-offer .24 at .26 they'd all look at each other in unspoken understanding. "Twenty-thirty!" The executing trader would sigh, knowing he was being fleeced, but what did he care? He maybe was an unleaded gas futures trader or a heating oil jockey just cleaning up some "blown-out" crude trader's mess for his clearing FCM. With a resigned voice he'd tap the outstretched hands: "Sell you a hundred...hundred... hundred...," until the inventory was cleared out. The traders squeaked with joy, just as the fish will whip themselves into a gorging froth when the much-anticipated bread hits the water. The FCM gopher would then move on to the next option in the ghost's position matrix, and the next, and the next, like a man generously passing out wads of hundred-dollar bills, until the liquidation was complete. Then he would go back to his normal round of business in his product.

They say "business is war," but I don't buy that. Only war is war. Losing some money doesn't rise to that level of trauma. I think only those who've never fought in a war would attempt to equate such a seminal experience with the buying and selling of a product or service, which is all business really is. But there is one similarity. In war men who are there one day are suddenly gone the next. Such was the case in trading too. Some traders may have stood in the same spot for months if not years but then ran into a streak of bad luck. Usually the losses compounded. Sometimes the traders tried to desperately "double up to even up." This often just accelerated the slide into ruin. In Hemingway's *The Sun Also Rises*, Mike Campbell is asked how he went bankrupt. "Two ways," Mike says. "Gradually and then suddenly." Such was usually the case in trading...but the day after Operation Desert Storm began was a notable exception. Several traders went straight to the "suddenly" part. And then just as suddenly, as in war, they were no longer there. Some of them were resilient enough to cobble together new stakes and come back to deal again. A few even rose from the ashes to become very successful traders in subsequent years. Others, however, were finished in the business, and I never saw them again. I heard one of them went from multimillionaire to working behind the counter for a rental-car company at Newark Airport, while another was employed at a ShopRite.

So there, again, was a lesson. The lord of the market is fickle. Always ... *always* live below your means. Especially in this business where your fortunes are often at the hands of crazed dictators who like to hang men from cranes for fun while holding your gas or heating oil tank hostage. As Winthorpe said: "*One minute you're up a half million in soybeans and the next, boom!*" You know the rest.

• • •

By the time Operation Desert Storm converted on February 24, 1991, to Operation Desert Sabre, the designation for the final land-based armored spearhead that raced over the Mideast sands to encircle and destroy Saddam's army, the war's outcome was a *fait accompli*. As General Powell coldly proclaimed when announcing his strategy for dealing with Iraq's exposed and devastated army: "First we're going to cut it off. Then we're going to kill it."

Oil prices returned to their prewar trading range, drifting from the high teens to the low twenties. Saddam did make good on his threats to launch SCUD missiles into Israel, but the tiny nation bit hard on its national pride and didn't retaliate, taking one for the team. There would be no Arab mutiny within the coalition. Even the criminal act of setting fire to Kuwait's oil fields, both as a punitive measure by Saddam aimed against his reviled creditors, as well as a final middle finger on the retreat by an Iraqi army in utter disarray and panic, did little to affect the supply of crude oil to the world. But it did create a cloud of dense black smoke looming over the battlefield, giving the conflict zone the aura of a Middle Eastern *Götterdämmerung*.

Thus energy prices stabilized and the immediate crisis passed into history. By the time the last of the oil fires were extinguished in November 1991 the threat to market continuity was long a thing of the past. The terrible loss of Iraqi lives, some 25,000 to 35,000 compared to the Coalition's mere 262 (half from noncombat accidents or friendly fire) as well as damage to the environment, was a tragic footnote.

We often ask why it is we seem to have selective outrage over which atrocities get our collective goats enough to mobilize for war to stop them. A million innocents are cleaved by machetes in Rwanda, and we do little but make Hollywood films about the slaughter. Christians are burned alive by Muslim fanatics in the Pashtun and the deserts of eastern Syria, and we talk tough and rattle our sabers but do little more. But a local pissant dictator runs tanks into an artificial nation of wealthy sheiks and suddenly the entire free world mobilizes. Why? The brutal reality of global relations is simple and direct. Where there is oil, the world's interest will follow.

Daniel Yergin in his tome *The Prize* explains why oil matters, and thus by default do those people who live in the oil-producing regions: "Ours has become a 'Hydrocarbon Society' and

we, in the language of anthropologists, 'Hydrocarbon Man.'...
Today we are so dependent on oil, and oil is so imbedded in our
daily doings, that we hardly stop to contemplate its pervasive
significance. It is oil that makes possible where we live, how we
live, how we commute to work, how we travel—even where we
conduct our courtships. It is the lifeblood of suburban commu-
nities. Oil (and natural gas) are the essential components in the
fertilizer on which world agriculture depends; oil makes it possible to transport food to the totally non-self-sufficient meg-
acities of the world. Oil also provides plastics and chemicals
that are the bricks and mortar of contemporary civilization, a
civilization that would collapse if the world's oil wells suddenly
went dry."

• • •

A year after my arrival in New York, my work was done. New
hires were brought on and Alan had matters well under control.
It was time for me to head back to the Chicago Merc and claim
my seat on the exchange as my door prize for helping Oscar
out. I was ready to trade Eurodollar options with the big boys.
I loaded up my new car, a Lilliputian Honda CRX, and headed
back to the Midwest; the New York skyline receded in my rearview mirror. But the energy bug had bitten me. I vowed that I
would learn what I could in Chicago and then return. There
were plenty more Saddam Husseins in that region of psychopa-
thy. Heck, even Saddam himself survived no worse for the wear
and went right back to pursuing one of his favorite pastimes:
gassing Kurds...while we shamefully did nothing to help them
after encouraging them to revolt. So long as sadistic madmen,

kleptocrats, and apocalyptic mullahs held their hands on the spigots of the most important commodity to the world, there would always be opportunity. I just didn't realize as I plotted my return how the eggs laid in this war would hatch in another and almost get me killed. Although with all that could have happened, I guess I'm one of the lucky ones. After all, I'm here to tell the story, aren't I? But first back to the city of big shoulders. And one of the worst days of my fledgling career.

CHAPTER 10

SUITING UP

In late summer 1991 I once again walked through the familiar heavy doors and onto the floor of the Chicago Merc, a little older and wiser—J. R. offered that I was more sarcastic and gritty as well—courtesy of the Big Apple. But this time I wasn't wearing my trusty yellow coat. Instead I sported the teal and navy-blue colors of a First Global options trader. Pinned to my jacket was the fabled blue square that I'd been working toward since I first set foot in this place two years before. My acronym was SCH. I was now a trader with all the opportunities and hazards this implied. In a way, it was like being stripped of a protective layer of expectation. What I mean is when I was a yellow-coat I'd shown "promise." I could go to sleep at night assuring myself that I would be a great trader if I ever got the chance. And someday that chance would come. But in the meantime, I just needed to hunker down behind Oscar and work hard and keep my shit together.

But now it was time to fulfill the promise. If I didn't do well, that was it. I would be done. Washed out. This was a lot of pressure I put on myself. Fortunately, I wasn't solely on my own. I was once again taken under the wing of a kindly brother and his partner, Max, as their junior trader. I would ease into it. Taking small positions and trying not to drain the account as I learned the ropes.

Max was one of my favorites. He wore thick glasses, his curly black hair fell long in the back in a style that reminded me of the comedian Sam Kinison, and like Kenny G from my ad days that seemed an eon ago, he gravitated toward the flamboyant aloha shirt. He was also "wicked smaht" as they say in Boston, with a very caustic wit. Like many Jews I've known with a wry sense of humor, he often cracked jokes about the Holocaust, not out of any disrespect, of course, but rather as an effective defense mechanism mastered by the likes of Mel Brooks to broach a subject so horrific it must be done obliquely and coated with a protective lacquer of jocularity. He thought it quite funny that his trading partner and friend, my brother, was a six-one chiseled light-haired man of knightly Germanic stock (Bavarian to be precise) who in another time and place would have been right at home manning the turret of a Tiger tank. Max's favorite joke was that my brother also had a relative who died in one of the concentration camps…"He fell out of the guard tower." Max was also a serious trader who never tired of reminding sloppy clerks, "This is real money!"

One's first trade on a grand exchange floor is the experience of plugging into something bigger than yourself. I somehow carved out enough real estate to stand beneath two main brokers. Being one of Oscar's crew gave me the perceived right to take a tiny sliver of space without having to fight for it. It was my task to cover this quadrant of the pit for my brother and Max. It had been a blind spot for them, and they were tired of missing orders coming in from that side of the floor just because of an accident of geography. The one broker was WULF, the squat fireplug of a man with a massive block for a head. The joke about him was to ask what would you rather have, a million dollars or Barry's head full of nickels? The other was a young, slim, and perpetually tanned dude (also favoring the colorful floral fashion of the islands) who wore his hair slicked straight back and tied off in a long ponytail. His badge was, appropriately, RKR for "Rocker," which we all called him. He reminded me in appearance of the author David Foster Wallace.

In this tiny space I called my "office," I would stand firm from 7:20 a.m. to 2:00 p.m. For roughly seven hours every day, five days a week, I would be elbowed and bumped and shoved and so crammed that I had to read my valuation sheets holding them just an inch from my eyes with my elbows tucked into my chest like I was praying. As with the crude ring, it was so jammed with bodies that we didn't stand side-by-side but rather chest-to-back. Such was the sardine nature of the pit that if one abruptly turned ninety degrees he would send a ripple down the line, like a shock wave, and a man five bodies farther down might pop off the step and fall to the floor.

Ding! When the bell rang on my first morning in the pit, and orders began to come in, I missed a quote request as I was still getting orientated. RKR had shouted out in his gruff, confident voice asking for something and all around me the mob raised their hands with all fingers extended shouting, "Five bid!" I had no clue what the order was, but I figured if all these experienced traders were shouting "five bid" then I'd better do the same. "Five bid!" I shouted like I meant it. Rocker went down the line 100...100...100...then to my surprise he pointed to me. "Hundred...welcome to the Eurodollars." I looked around to peek at what the trader next to me was carding up to see what

I'd just done. To my surprise I'd just paid 35 ticks for a June 95.50 call. They would soon trade again at 36 and then 37 and I sold out fifty at each level making $3,750 for the team. Would that it were always this easy.

JFS, a trader who'd been in the options pit for years and stood on that coveted top step with Oscar, was a kindly math whiz. He was an unassuming character you'd never know was worth millions. From his vantage point he saw and catalogued everything that went on in the pit. He was *very* sharp. I think he got a kick out of watching my first day. "Little Shafe!" I heard him shout to me from his perch after I carded up my second fifty-lot sale. I looked over to see him throw me a thumbs-up. "How'd you like those calls?" He was happy that my first trade was a winner.

I was in the trading scene now. But after that it would take time to become one of "the boys." There was a pecking order, and though no longer a yellowcoat, I was a rookie trader and hadn't yet earned the right to be in on all the good trades. Some of these people had been doing favors for the brokers for years, and there was a trust built up through times when a broker may have miscounted and even though it cost the trader money, he would take a deal that was already against him so the broker wouldn't eat the error. The broker then would return the favor by giving him an extra helping of the next prime trade to come along. During my first month WULF, who was old-school Merc, would often get a nice order and divvy them up to the outstretched hands like Father Christmas visiting an orphanage. But when he'd get to my hand, he'd say, "Not yet," and move on with no trade for me.

Although in many ways I was treated like a neophyte, I was still a familiar enough presence by then that the traders had no qualms about ribbing me when it was justified. One weekend I made the mistake of overdoing it with the Sun-In hair lightening product to the point where my usually dark brown lid was a curious, and obvious, reddish blond. When I stepped into the options pit that Monday morning, I was slammed with a tsunami of merciless mockery. It being a slow day, my brother orchestrated a "Little Shafe's Hair Poetry Contest." The challenge was to describe in just one sentence his little brother's newly dyed mane with as much poetic flourish as possible. Entries came in from all over—even the old tobacco-chewing cattle traders in their Olathe boots from the far side of the exchange submitted something related to a horse's forelock. The three finalists were: second runner up, "*A dollop of auburn delight.*" Taking silver was "*A lolling coif of gossamer locks,*" and the winner, penned by my brother himself, "*A sartorial swirl of strawberry splendor.*" (I think his was the best as he captured not only the majesty of my new look, but also the magical color transformation that had taken place.)

There may have been an uneasy camaraderie among the traders in the pits, but in the end, we were there, as Oscar said, to make money, not friends. We were competitors, and as such little mercy was shown to this piece of fresh meat. I had to be careful as I knew I was as enticing a target to the seasoned traders as a vulnerable wildebeest calf is to a pack of hyenas. I discovered this the hard way when Barry asked for a market and for whatever reason others were too occupied hedging a trade just finished to bother. Here was my chance to get in WULF's good graces. I looked at my sheets, promptly read the wrong month, and made him a market. I was off by four ticks, $100 per contract, and in no time two traders from across the pit saw what I'd done and flashed Barry to sell me five hundred each for them. They picked me off. To his credit Barry sold me only twenty-five apiece. "Make sure you quote March next time," he said. "This is as close to a Mulligan as I'll give you." It was a $5,000 lesson…but thanks to Barry taking some pity on me it wasn't a $100,000 lesson! He didn't protect me just to be Captain Sunshine. Oscar, he realized, saw the whole thing go down from his crow's nest on the top step and was glaring back and forth between WULF and the two predators who tried to jam me with "wood", as we called sizeable trades. Another rule of life: it helps to have powerful friends.

This trade did serve to drive home to me the fact that, à la Max, this was "real money," and I still had a lot to learn. There was no value in being fast if I was wrong. But I took my loss like a man. The older guys especially didn't want to hear a young punk like me bitching at the injustice of it all. GGE ("Go Get 'Em"), an irascible, goggle-eyed snapping turtle of a man, and one of my favorite old-guard traders, had a go-to retort whenever I'd whine about missing my futures on a hedge or just doing a trade that went against me: "You really should complain, Little Shafe, because that's the first time that's ever happened here." Fair point.

By the end of my first month I'd grown confident enough to be more forceful. And the brokers were starting to see me as one of their gang. But I still had to watch myself. There were a few brokers who, like Tom Hagen in *The Godfather*, serviced just one client. Usually they filled for one of the biggest traders in the markets who'd call in from their desks upstairs or in New

York and put on an enormous speculative position...legendary dealers like George Soros, Paul Tudor Jones, Bruce Kovner, Richard Dennis, and the like. An interesting duo were two brothers who were short, round, and bald...we likened them to the toy Weebles (because they "wobble but won't fall down"). They wore bright purple jackets, and you didn't see them very often. But when they did appear on the floor, whether in our pit or one of the many others in which their bosses were active, the market-makers were both excited and wary. If one of these guys popped up on the top step of our pit, we knew they weren't coming in to trade small. So we had to make sure the prices we showed had enough embedded "edge" to absorb a massive wave of buys or sales.

When one of the twins stepped into the options crowd and asked for a bid on a call worth 46 ticks, we all screamed, "Forty-four bid!" (2 ticks below value). He banged out ten thousand calls like a machine gun, and the pit detonated with frantic options traders all around whirling and flashing hedging orders to their futures clerks. To my chagrin, I didn't get any. What the hell? As I was farthest away from him, I thought the "purple people eater," as the clerks called him, didn't see me. I began screaming in righteous indignation. "Hey, Mister! I was four bid! *Four bid*!" I wasn't so anxious to buy the options as to make a point. I thought he was finished. He looked up from carding his trades, fixed me with an icy glare, crossed his forearms, making an "X," and pushed them toward me in a gesture I recognized as wood and shouted, "Sell you *a thousand*! You want more?"

Stunned, I said with a suddenly dry mouth: "No, I'm good, thanks."

"I bet you are. Now shut the hell up!" Then he disappeared before I could ask him to only make it a hundred. I owned them now.

Shit....

To my horror I realized the calls I'd begged for him to jam down my throat had a .50 delta ... I was suddenly exposed to the equivalent of being long 500 futures. I desperately yelled at one of my clerks, "June sell five hundred!" At that exact moment the futures popped 2 ticks, and I was able to sell them at a great level. I'd just booked a $25,000 winner. Somehow through the noise I could hear the ever-observant JFS call to my brother, "Hey, Shafe, your kid brother just took down a thousand lot." My brother looked over to me and mouthed, "What'd you do?" I flashed him the details and after he did the quick math in his head, he feigned wiping his brow in relief. I even saw Oscar smile. I'd arrived. You've got to pay your dues throughout life in any new endeavor, and a badge is only that. A badge. It's how you handle that badge that earns respect.

Sometimes that respect is earned not in how you take in a winner but deal with a disastrous loser. Not long after my being nearly gutted by the Weeble, I saw how taking down such size could also lead to calamity in an unnervingly quick period of time. And you didn't have to walk into the pits long oil in the midst of a Persian Gulf war to be scythed down by the reaper of terrible timing. Like those pesky gum bombs, financial landmines in all forms were sprinkled about the trading floors and could blow you to bits before you even knew you'd stepped on one. Ours came in the form of the dreaded "clerk error." And it almost wiped us out.

CHAPTER 11

40,000 TICKS

EVERY MONTH THE CENSUS BUREAU would release a report
on the previous month's Advance Monthly Sales for Retail and
Food Services. This figure was known on the trading floor simply as "Retail Sales." This was one of those "numbers" that was
released at 7:30 a.m., just ten minutes into the trading session,
and provided another pixel in the always-adjusting picture of
the health of the US economy, and thus the potential direction
of future interest rates. Before any significant number came out,
usually one of two things occurred. Either the floor would be
relatively quiet, as no one wanted to take a position just before
a potentially market-moving piece of news came out and get
caught flatfooted. Or a series of large orders within minutes
prior to any announcement would hit the floor. These usually
came from the institutional dealers in offices in New York or
Chicago or London. Sometimes they gave away good value
because they were merely trying to exit their exposure before
the data release, or "be flat going into the number." But other
times they were actually taking on a large position...because
they knew something. The number may have already been
leaked to them, even. And you never knew which it was, so you
had to be wary.

For example: at around 2:00 p.m. on November 9, 2012, there was a surge of massive put buying (bearish positions) against the stock of megacompany Lockheed Martin Corp. On a typical trading day in 2012 just over nine hundred put options in the generally healthy company would trade. But on this day, all at once roughly *fifty-seven thousand* puts changed hands. Sure enough, a little later in the afternoon came word that the company's COO (who was slated to be named CEO by the end of the year) abruptly resigned over a scandal involving a "close personal relationship" with a subordinate. I'm sure it was just a coincidence, said the man last seen exiting the realtor's office with the deed to the Brooklyn Bridge in his hand.

And so it was that on a Retail Sales day in February of 1992, at barely one minute before 7:30 a.m., a large bullish order hit the Eurodollar options pit on my brother's side. I looked over and saw him and those around him suddenly start hopping and motioning frantically as if someone just poured boiling water all over the traders in his quadrant. What he'd just done was take down a very large clip of options at once. He sold two thousand calls and bought two thousand puts in December simultaneously,[4] which was a very bearish play (the other side being the opposite view and thus very bullish, obviously). It wasn't the size of the options block per se which was so dicey. Two thousand cars, though nothing to scoff at, wasn't an unheard-of trade in the Eurodollars by this time. It was that it had a .90 delta and was a back-month trade; in other words, in order to lock in his profit (which was hefty as there were tens of thousands of dol-

---

4   This highly directional strategy was known in the Eurodollar options pit as a "squash" but more commonly called a "fence."

lars of edge in both the puts he bought for a discount and calls he sold at a premium) my brother had to very quickly communicate to the back-months clerk all the way on the most distant edge of the futures pit a buy of 1,800 December futures (2,000 times .90) in the next thirty seconds before the number hit. He didn't have time to go through the front-month clerk who would then relay it. As such, he waved his arms frantically until he caught the eye of the FGT clerk far away on the other side of the futures pit and sharply flashed the order.

"*Dec! Buy Eighteen Hundred!*"

The clerk acknowledged the order and shouted down to Oscar's gifted back-months trader, Jaimo, who filled FGT options hedge orders as part of Oscar's seat sponsorship deal. "Jaimo!" he shouted. JAM turned and looked up at him. The clerk flashed while yelling, "Dec! Buy Eighteen Hundred!" Jaimo checked the clock and, understanding the urgency given the number about to hit the tape, quickly scooped up 1,800 December futures at a great level to lock in the profit. A huge winner!

Then it all fell apart....

My brother, wishing to make sure the clerk was indeed working his order correctly, flashed up to him. "*CHECKING* (the same hand signal you make to a waiter when you ask for the bill) ... *working* (a twirl of the finger) *to buy eighteen hundred Dec!*"

Unfortunately, the clerk was busy confirming the 1,800-lot fill with Jaimo and had taken his eye off the options pit for at most five seconds. When he looked back up again all his eyes caught was the tail end of my brother's message. He'd missed the confirmation part. All he read was: *"... buy eighteen hundred Dec!"*

The clerk misread this as an order to double the trade and buy *another* 1,800 futures just seconds before the announcement. He naturally assumed that whatever occurred way over there in the options pit just went down again. So, he dutifully called down to Jaimo. "Hey! Dec. Buy another eighteen hundred! Total *all day* thirty-six hundred!" ("All day" being vernacular for the full size of an order.)

Once again JAM quickly filled the order with seconds to spare before the number came out. It was, in fact, rather easy to buy so many futures at this moment, which gave him pause.

My brother then pleaded with the clerk. *"Am I filled?"*

The clerk gave him the thumbs up. *"Filled! Filled!"* When he reported the price, my brother leaped for joy. It was a huge winner. Other traders patted him on the back for having the brass in the pants to trade so large just before a number came out in the less liquid December contract with such a high delta to cover. All in a day's work, he smiled, feeling suitably proud. He would not have been smiling had he known he was going into the Retail Sales number "naked" (unhedged) long 1,800 futures.

When the number came out it was heavily bearish, and the market reacted violently. It plummeted twenty ticks, taking 1,800 of my brother's naked longs at $25.00 per tick down with it. But no one knew this yet.

It wasn't until the clerk flashed over the details of the trade that my brother's face went ashen. He was tallying up the fills and to his horror the clerk was reporting to him on his 3,600

December futures bought at a level twenty ticks higher than where we were now trading post-number.

"*Thirty-six hundred? You mean eighteen hundred,*" my brother flashed and mouthed with great emphasis for clarity.

"*No. You said to buy another eighteen hundred,*" the clerk flashed back. "*I know thirty-six hundred all day.*"

For a second it was as if time stood still. Then the realization hit like a cannonball. In that instant, triumph turned to catastrophe. It happens that quickly. The most banal of actions, like briefly glancing down to check a tally, can be so devastating in its impact if timed poorly as to seem absurd. In this clerk's case, a conscientious act of checking a total turned disastrous when he looked back over to the options pit and intercepted the second half of the flashed message, misconstruing an instruction to confirm he was buying 1,800 December futures with an order to buy 1,800 *more*.

No doubt the clerk felt his insides go hollow when he both realized what happened and then glanced up at the board to see EDZ2 -22, EDZ2 being the commodities code for December 1992 Eurodollars, when it had just been unchanged before the Retail Sales report came out. A loss of 22 ticks on 1,800 lots amounted to just shy of $1,000,000. He had the unenviable task of making the long walk over to the options pit to confirm with my brother and Max: "I think we overbought eighteen hundred Dec."

"You think? Or you know?" asked Max, whose mouth suddenly went dry.

"I know." At that point Max looked up at the board that showed EDZ2 -22, and he fought off a wave of nausea. My brother tried to show a brave face, but his usually healthy tan pallor had gone wet and colorless.

Once it was confirmed that there had, indeed, been a massive overbuy, my brother immediately instructed another clerk in the back-months to dump the 1,800 longs, locking in a $990,000 hit, before the loss could get even worse. Which is the only thing to do when you have an error. Get out immediately no matter how painful, as it can always go even more against you. I've seen guys hang on to small positions put on by mistake hoping the market will come back and spare them from taking a loss, only to watch a small mistake grow exponentially more expensive as the price action just continues to go against them.

I was blissfully unaware of any of this as I was concentrating on the orders from WULF and RKR in my immediate front. It's like being in a pitched battle and you're only cognizant of what's happening in your immediate sector of the line, unaware that the flanks have been turned and you need to retreat. It wasn't until I spied my brother slinking back into the options pit white as Gollum that I suspected something was amiss.

He looked at me and then slowly flashed to me the message: "*We just got fucked out of forty thousand ticks.*"

When he pulled his earlobe with his thumb and forefinger in the arb signal for "ticks" I thought he meant something else as forty thousand ticks made no sense. So, I replied, "*Forty thousand dollars?*" and rubbed my thumb to my index and middle fingers in the universal symbol of cash. His face suddenly flashed crimson as might a startled cuttlefish. "*Ticks!*" he screeched and practically ripped off his earlobe for emphasis in case I had no doubt that what we were talking about wasn't forty grand—which was bad enough—but *twenty-five times that amount.* At the time, one million dollars was more money than I'd ever imagined I could make in a year. To *lose* that much in less than ten seconds was utterly mind-boggling to me. As the indifferent banker in *South Park* might say: "Aaaand it's gone!"

Needless to say, neither my brother, Max, nor their young junior here were in much of a mindset to trade any more that day. How do you recover from such a severe gut punch? Most of the remainder of the day was spent trying to explain what happened to Oscar, who'd been too busy with his own whirlwind of dealing to notice what happened. Just one of those things, really. Whaddya gonna do?

Oscar took it in stride as much as one can. None of his rules had been violated, so he couldn't do anything punitive. Even the clerk really hadn't done anything wrong. It wasn't like he was flipping through a *Hustler* magazine when the trade went down and thus missed my brother's full signal through negligence. If anything, he was diligently making sure the original order as he saw it was being filled as he was well aware of how little time he had. He just looked up a second too late. One second was all it took to obliterate a trading account.

The clerk still felt bad nonetheless and would, in fact, lose his job over this. This was unfair. But lesson number whatever from the floor: life isn't always fair. Before he knew his fate, he tried to apologize when the trading day was done and the shock of the moment had given way to the dull throb of regret. My brother struggled to be philosophical. At least whoever the shark was who took the other bullish side of his option trade got the snot kicked out of him when the market freefell after the number. He felt a bit like a jumper who'd grabbed someone by the sleeve and taken him plummeting to his death for the ride. "It's no big deal," he then said to the clerk; the sarcasm dripping from his lips was so acidic it burned a hole in the floor. "Just think of it as buying twenty Porsche 928s, lining them up on Navy Pier, and one by one we push them over the side into Lake Michigan." Although I can understand my brother's frustrations, he should have known better, as that was a violation of a cardinal rule of trading. Never quantify with real purchases what your losses could have bought you. Don't ever say: "I lost ten grand today. That's a nice vacation!" It will prevent you from taking the necessary risk you must be willing to accept to succeed in trading. Therefore, you must think of your account as a scorecard. Fluctuating numbers, with no meaning beyond just that. Otherwise, the "what I could have done with that" will drive you mad. And you will never survive.

Max's approach was more original, if crueler. He took out a wad of bills from his pocket and thrust them into the hapless clerk's trembling, pasty hand. "Here," he said with a crocodile smile. "I want you to go out tonight and don't worry about anything. Go for drinks, a nice meal—hell, if there's any leftover, find yourself a girl and get laid."

"Hey, thanks, Max," the relieved clerk said. "I appreciate the understanding. I feel terrible."

"I know you do," said Max. "Oh, and then when you're done," he added almost as an afterthought, "I want you to go up to the roof of your building and seriously consider killing yourself." Max walked away, leaving a stunned clerk to look at me searching for any kind of redemption. I had none to give.

That soon-to-be-canned clerk is now one of Chicago's top commercial real estate brokers, and my guess is he did better in his career than I have in mine, so good on him. Again, the dots connect backward.

Max went home to work on restoring his classic 1966 Lincoln Continental to clear his mind. I took my frustrations out at the gym, watched a *Simpsons* tape to try and laugh, and then slept the troubled, shallow sleep of the anxious. My brother, on the other hand, went on a full-scale sixth gear with M-drive turbo bender. The Eurodollar pit closed at 2:00 p.m., and by 3:00 p.m., he was pounding shot after shot at The Lodge on Division Street, which was his favorite hangout. By the time most normal people were leaving work his needle was fully in the red. At one point, he stumbled blindly into a Mercedes dealership and stood swaying in the showroom as he visually absorbed the collection of shiny luxury vehicles that seemed to be mocking his earlier Porsche comment. (Luckily for the pur-veyors of Stuttgart's most famous product there were no such dealers in the immediate vicinity.) At the top of his consider-ably powerful lungs he screamed to the stunned customers and salesmen in the showroom: "My clerk pissed away every one of these goddamned cars today!" Then he fell back outside onto the street under the Windy City's cold February sunlight. Once again, the art of the film *Trading Places* was imitated by real life. All that my drunken brother was missing in his blind stupor was the intoxicated Winthorpe's Santa Claus suit and stolen salmon stuck to the beard. At one point my brother was face down on the sidewalk and would later recall in vivid detail the sight of well-polished wingtips passing by his field of vision. Was this a skid row bum at their feet? No, just one of the captains of high finance on the floor of one of the most prestigious commodi-ties exchanges in the world.

Later that day, a concerned Max went out and, knowing his favorite drinking spots, tracked down his toasted trading partner who was stumbling along the street. My brother collected himself and they went out for Mexican in an area we called "The Viagra Triangle" because the bars in that neighborhood were known for younger girls, aspiring models and the like, who in turn lured gray-haired, wealthy sugar daddies into their honey-traps. The self-pitying boozing continued well into the night. Max foolishly tried to drive my brother home and his weaving car was promptly pulled over by the Chicago Police. Both he and my brother found themselves standing spread-eagle with palms planted on the hood of a CPD cruiser being frisked. The flashing lights reflecting on their dejected and severely buzzed faces showed the day had gone from bad to worse. Then, this being Chicago, the police radio crackled with an APB alerting them of a shooting in progress. The cops lost all interest in the two drunken traders. "This is your lucky day, ladies," an officer sneered as he tossed the keys into Max's car and locked all the doors before slamming them shut.

• • •

Our clerk was, of course, not the first or the last to ever make an error based on a misunderstanding rather than any gross negligence…even if Max suggested after the fact that he end his life in some Bushido gesture of atonement. Mistakes were common across all trading floors, and some were almost laughable. There's the story of the clerk on the COMEX who was on the phone with a gold trader for a Hong Kong bank. When you had a man for whom Cantonese and Mandarin were his first and second languages, with English a distant third, and a kid from Staten Island who almost failed high school English despite it being his mother tongue, trying to make sense of each other over the din of screaming and ambient noise through a phone line that stretched eight thousand miles, something was bound to happen. As the story goes the trader called the clerk and told him to buy June gold futures. When the clerk asked him how many he needed the man curtly responded in painfully broken English: "Ahhhyouwann!"

"Wait, how many?" the clerk asked him again.

"Ahhhyouwann!" the testy Chinese trader repeated.

"All you want?" said the clerk, trying to confirm that the man was putting in a massive buy order.

"*Ahhhyouwann!*" the irate trader screamed again over the line.

Sensing the urgency, and assuming the trader on the other side of the globe where it was already thirteen hours ahead knew some bit of news that hadn't hit the tape yet, the phone clerk dutifully obliged. He shouted from his grungy booth over to his broker's arb clerk and signaled him to start buying June gold at the market price, no limit.

"*Size?*" the arb clerk mouthed while patting the top of his head.

"Just start buyin' 'em, Franky!" the phone clerk yelled so the arb clerk could hear him. So could everyone else and they converged on the broker who started lifting every June gold offer he could lay his hands on. This surge of buying sent the market for not just gold but all precious metals screaming to new highs on the day. Someone knew something. It wouldn't be the first time. Traders like Michael Marcus made a fortune in 1979 when the news hit some desks but not others that the Russians invaded Afghanistan and loaded up on gold futures before metals started surging. This kind of unlimited buying coming in from an Asian bank felt like a setup, but the levels the broker was paying were too rich to pass up for those who may have been long already and looking for an opportunity to unwind with a tidy profit. Even though they suspected they were leaving money on the table, they saw this as a classic situation in which to practice one of the holy commandments of commodities trading: get out when you *can*, not when you *must*.

"Yo, I got you eight hundred so far, but I gotta get an actual number!" the arb clerk flashed and screamed at the booth simultaneously in exasperation.

"Sir, I need a firm number," the phone clerk shouted above the chaos into the handset. "We got you eight hundred and buying more, but what exactly is the amount you need please?"

The panicked voice now hollered. "Nooo! I say ahhhyouwann!"

"Right," said the clerk. "I'm trying to get you all you want but I need an actual amount or we'll just be buying gold all day 'til I start rippin' off jewelry in there."

At that point the Chinese trader's British manager came on the line and with a very perturbed but professional voice said calmly: "He's good for now, mate. What's the count?"

The clerk immediately shouted to the floor, "Out! Franky, out! Out!" Then when the buying ceased he reported the fills. The bank had ended up with exactly one thousand long June gold futures at a level that averaged in slightly better than where it was trading. "Okay, mate," said the manager. "You can try and sell nine hundred and ninety-nine as best you can, not held."

The clerk paused in confusion before saying: "I'm confirming. You now want to *sell* all but one back out?"

"That's right," said the dealer. "He was trying to tell you that his size was 'only one.' He just needs a one-lot. Slight miscommunication there, eh? We'll handle it on our end. Cheers." The overseas bank may have even ended up making a small profit given the way his "all you want" had muscled the thin metals market higher. Strange things could and would happen.

• • •

We took small comfort in the fact that we were not the only victims of a cruel twist of fate in a business practically inviting such errors. ("That's the first time that's ever happened here." Yeah, yeah.) The next day, Wednesday, everyone walked into the office and Roselyn grimly handed us the P&L from the day before. The account was depleted by $890,000. As it turned out, my brother's original trade had been a 4,000-tick winner, so the error had been cut by one hundred thousand. Added to that, we were already up a million on the year, so the account was now essentially slashed to a quarter stick. Several months' hard work nearly wiped out. With that wonderful good morning we made our way down to the trading floor. Sympathetic eyes followed us as we took our positions in the pit. When the bell rang, we did what we were supposed to do. We made markets and traded. I noticed the brokers were being especially generous to me in the way they divvied up the choicest trades, and no one around me bitched too hard at them. And to think it only took paying a nine-hundred-thousand-dollar entrance fee to be admitted into the club.

But none of the three of us were really trading well. Our minds just weren't in it. The math came slowly to me. Even with RKR's and WULF's generosity I was trading poorly. And this was when I learned another lesson about surviving the trading game. Sometimes it takes more discipline to call it quits for the day and take a dive than stay in the ring and get pummeled again and again, adding to your losses. I know one desk manager for a major bank who literally walked over to one of his star traders who, for whatever reason, was losing money. And yet the trader insisted on trying to recoup his losses by entering the ol' "double-up-to-even-up" death spiral. The manager literally knelt down behind the man's desk and unplugged his computer. It was my brother, older, wiser, brutally hungover from his revival at the Mercedes dealership but recovered enough to think more clearly than I, who pulled me away and suggested we grab an early lunch at the Merc Club and call it a day. Sounded good to me.

Heads bowed in weariness, we made our way off the exchange, leaving Max the good sport to mind the store. More than one trader told us it took a lot of character to step back in just one day after what happened, but what else were we supposed to do? You can't make it back if you don't trade.

We sidled up to the empty bar overlooking the river, and a rather cute bartender with big dimples and dark, gonna-getcha eyes drifted over and slid two menus in front of us. We must have looked like hell because she said: "Tough day, guys?"

"Tough week," my brother said. I buried my face in the cocktail menu.

"That bad, huh?"

I smiled wanly and channeled Cal. "Like you read about."

She nodded sympathetically. "What'll ya have?"

She took our orders and poured two beers from the tap. As she brought them over to us she caught the vibe that we really were very sullen and dejected. So, she did what bartenders do. She tried to cheer us up.

"Hey, boys," she said in a soothing voice. "You may have had a tough day, but it can always be worse."

"It can?" I asked incredulously.

"Sure." She leaned in as if about to let us in on a delicious secret. "I heard that just yesterday some poor guys lost a million dollars because of a clerk error. Now that," she insisted, "is a bad day."

She patted us each on the forearm and moved on with a big smile on her face, confident that her *schadenfreude* approach to motivational speaking had had the desired effect. I was too stunned to say anything. But my brother, again showing his five years on me, let slip a staccato chuckle. "Sure would suck to be those guys." He then ordered up two shots of tequila. It seemed like the right thing to do.

CHAPTER 12

NYMEX 2.0 AND A BOMB

ALTHOUGH SUCH AN ERROR WAS devastating as much to our
morale as to our financial futures—we were still in our ear-
ly-to-mid-twenties after all—a more ominous development
regarding our chosen profession was coming into being. In retrospect, it signified the most sweeping and radical overhaul of
my business... and no less than the beginning of the end of the
open outcry methodology that had been in place since the first
futures exchange was established in Chicago 144 years earlier.
In the 1990s the floor personnel were like the passengers on the
Titanic. Although they may have felt just a slight tremble from
the hull's brush up against the killer iceberg, very few of them
realized that the vessel had just suffered a mortal blow and even
as they steamed ahead, the holds below deck were taking on
water. The iceberg that would sink the century-and-a-half trading floor tradition was the advent of technology.

On June 25, 1992, CME Globex went live. It was an online
platform that allowed dealers to bypass the floor and trade
directly with each other by mouse click. Initial volumes were
modest, but interest was keen, and the system grew steadily
in popularity. While the program was initially sold as a con-
venience for currency traders, CME Group leadership had a

larger vision and believed that electronic trading could be made to serve as another source of distribution for all the exchange's varied product lines. As far as the floor was concerned, the enemy had arrived.

• • •

Meanwhile, just as the electronic kraken was being unshackled, I found myself back in lower Manhattan, once again standing on the grungy NYMEX trading floor. This time I was in New York to stay. Personal reasons compelled my return to the Big Apple. I'd met my future wife while in New York working under Alan during the Gulf War. After a long-distance romance, I decided I wanted to come back to the East Coast and build a life with the future Mrs. Lil' Shafe.

Things had changed workwise too. Oscar sent my brother out to Singapore to trade the mushrooming Euroyen contract. I felt that was the signal to move away from his shadow and start fresh on a new exchange where I was not Lil' Shafe (or "Fredo" as some called me in reference to Michael Corleone's less charismatic brother) but rather badge SCH. So I headed east again. It was a decision that almost cost me my life.

• • •

In 1993, the NYMEX floor was as I'd remembered it, although some of the faces had changed. The losers in the Gulf War had been purged while I was still there. The winners of that war, the "Gulf War babies" if you recall, worked less than they used to but still came in. One broker I'd always liked ("It's war, I tell ya!")

was still plugging away just as I'd remembered him. He sometimes did his FCM favors by filling tiny orders we assumed were retail customers coming in to trade. Needless to say, he couldn't be bothered with the occasional odd-lot phoned in from some Sarasota dentist trying his hand at futures trading in between extractions, so he filled them quickly. And the mini-speculators sold them cheap and paid dear for the privilege of participating in markets best left to the professionals. He'd announce his juicy little order with his customary: "All right, ya filthy animals! Who wants to rip off the widows and orphans today?" He had good reason to be jovial…ever since the Gulf War put the NYMEX on the map, the volume in energy futures and options was growing "bigly," as he observed.

The FGT office had also grown. There were more personnel now, and they'd moved to a larger office to accommodate the steady growth in futures and options volumes not just in crude oil trading but the entire energy complex, which also included natural gas, heating oil, and unleaded gas—the latter two, collectively known as "crude products" as they were oil distillates, would be my new hunting ground. So I was no longer a Eurodollar jockey. I was now an energy trader.

Every product I traded throughout my career had its own idiosyncrasies, behavioral patterns, and unique characteristics. Thus, no matter how experienced you were in the markets, there was always a learning curve. But one common aspect among any exchange floor, whether trading Eurodollars in Chicago or distillates in New York, were the painful stretches of tedium that were as much the rule as the exception. There were times when nothing was happening. Some sat down—eating as well as sitting was permitted on the NYMEX floor—and read paperbacks, did crossword puzzles, perused the gossip pages, or just chatted about matters unrelated to the markets. Although it might have seemed like a waste of time to some, good traders understood a cardinal rule: when there's nothing to do, do nothing. Otherwise, in listless markets with no clear direction, you could find yourself "churning," trading with no sound plan, and just transferring money from your account to your brokers' and FCM's in commissions.

During such languid periods, the New York crew could be just as merciless in the gag department as their Chicago cousins. One clerk for a large brokerage firm was known for religiously playing the lottery, and constantly informing us of what he would do if he won, including whom he would tell to "go fuck themselves." Not surprisingly, he made himself as much a target as a man who climbs out of the trenches and dares the enemy to take a shot at him. He always kept his lottery tickets in an envelope in his floor coat. So the day after a big drawing in which nobody won, one of his coworkers looked up the winning drawing from the night before and promptly bought a ticket with those numbers on it. Then he found the man's jacket hanging in the office upstairs and stuffed it in the envelope among the others before the mark arrived for work. Later that day on the floor, the target clerk casually checked yesterday's winning numbers against the tickets in his pocket. Half the energy pits were in on the joke and all watched his expression change from confusion, to hope, to euphoria as he screamed out, "I won! I fuckin' won the lottery!" They let him hoot and howl and high-five anyone he could corner and show the "winning" ticket to for about ten minutes. It was when he announced that he was going to march up to the brokerage main office and quit, but not before he told his manager what he *really* thought of him, that some of the other clerks had to practically tackle the deluded man as he stormed off the floor and give him the bad news that his winning ticket was for the next drawing, not last night's. The poor schmuck went from jubilation to despondency to a rage against any and all who'd been in on the gag and thus so cruel as to give him a taste of wealth beyond his wildest dreams only to dash his joy against the rocks of a practical joke that arose solely from others' boredom. But at least the jokesters didn't let him torpedo his career. Call it a rare show of mercy from the floor. (Ironically, or sadistically if you prefer, a broker in the products options pit soon after actually *did* win a lottery drawing and bought a nice house on the Jersey Shore with the proceeds.)

Also as with Chicago, gambling often filled the void during blocks of prolonged lethargy. One of the most popular activities was during March Madness, when traders bought and sold NCAA futures just like they would commodities futures… albeit these were generally, ahem, frowned upon by the IRS. In fact, the gambling on college basketball had become so widespread that a former NYMEX director once told me the exchange fielded an inquiry from the FBI.

Trading March Madness futures was pretty straightforward. It was based on odds. At the beginning of the tournament with the round of sixty-four you could buy or sell any team. If there was a long shot with maybe 30:1 odds they'd capture the championship then you might've sold them at $100 and hoped they lost early and you kept the $100, like an option expiring worthless. If you thought they had a chance to do well you might've bought them knowing the most you'd lose is how much you paid. Like buying an option. If they did somehow win then you would collect \$3,100 (30÷1 x 100 + 100). After each round, the pool of teams was whittled down, and so the survivors' values swelled as their odds of winning increased. If the longshot team survived into the round of thirty-two, you might then have opted to sell them out as now they'd be trading at a higher level of maybe \$200...but you thought they couldn't make it to the next round so you were happy to collect your profit. What you did *not* want to happen was to keep selling them outright just to collect the premium expecting them to be eliminated only to watch them keep advancing until they somehow miraculously took home the championship. Then you'd have to pay everyone you sold to the full value of \$3,100 per sale, less whatever small premium you originally received.

The problem with NCAA futures is that they really could bankrupt a man—especially an already impoverished clerk making less than minimum wage if you ran the per-hour numbers. My clerk, Leonid, whose parents were Russian citizens, so he spoke the language fluently, was heavily involved in the NCAA futures trading ring. Believing an upset was coming (it had already happened to the favored Duke) he continued to sell North Carolina as the tournament progressed. He sold and sold and sold as they advanced, growing ever more anxious as the Tarheels rampaged from the Sweet Sixteen to the Elite Eight to the Final Four and finally the Championship game itself. By the opening tip-off of the 1993 final, Lenny, as he was called, was in hock to various traders and other clerks in the combined amount of some \$60,000. North Carolina beat Michigan 77–71, and the next day my clerk never showed up for work. I have an image of Lenny frantically dialing the airlines right after Michigan's double-teamed Chris Webber tried to call a timeout with eleven seconds on the clock and his team down by two, but, as they had none remaining, he got hit with a technical foul instead, sealing the Wolverines' and my clerk's dooms. I finally got a call from the AWOL Russian that afternoon. Quite unexpectedly, he said, he got a "great opportunity" to go work for his uncle in Volgograd...thanks for all your support, Shafe, and see you around. Although I couldn't be sure, it sounded like he was calling from a payphone in an airport terminal as I thought I heard flight arrivals and departure announcements in the muffled background.

I had no clue about my fugitive clerk's gambling debts until the more hard-looking unibrowed clerks for the oil futures traders to whom he'd sold many a Tarheel came looking for him. "Shafe, you seen Lenny?" they'd ask in Joe Pesci–like Brooklyn or Staten Island accents. "He quit," I told one after another. "Guy's in Russia now. Can you believe that? You know a clerk looking for a job?"

"Russia! Dat mothafuckah ran out on us!" they'd snarl. "He owes Bobby (or Jimmy and Tony or whomever) ten Gs in Carolina!" Then they'd let me know that "if dat punk ever shows his face in dese pits again he's gonna be snorkelin' da Hudson, without no snorkel, know what I'm sayin'?" They really said that. The New York guys made the Chicago traders sound like Tony Blair.

Another clerk in natural gas loved to gamble on football, college and professional, although not in the destructive way of the now-fugitive Leonid. He read the sports pages religiously. But he would often find himself on an extended losing streak to the point where I thought it was distracting him from work… at least on the Monday following a particularly punishing weekend.

"I swear, Shafe, I can't catch a break," he moaned to me. "Every bet I made, I mean every fuckin' team, no matter what I did, bettin' on the spread, the over-under, whatever, and I fuckin' lost. You believe dat? Goin' on five weeks in a row now."

"You ever think about betting on a sport other than football?" I suggested innocently. "Like maybe switch to college hoops or something? You know, to mix it up?"

He looked at me as if that was the stupidest suggestion he'd ever heard. "Why the fuck would I do that? I don't know shit about basketball."

• • •

Within a few weeks of my return to New York, someone tried to kill me. Well, not me in particular but rather everyone in the buildings in which I worked as well as the surrounding neighborhood.

On Friday, February 26, 1993, at around noon, I took a break from a quiet Friday and left the trading floor. I rode the little elevator down to the lobby and casually strolled the indoor promenade that connected the WTC buildings in a below-ground mall lined with retail shops and eateries. At that exact moment, a psychotic named Ramzi Yousef and his Jordanian friend, Eyad Ismoil, pulled a yellow Ryder van into the parking garage underneath the 110-story Tower One and parked it on level B-2. Stuffed inside the cab of the rental truck was a makeshift urea nitrate-hydrogen gas bomb weighing 1,336 pounds. Just as I was lazily strolling the shops, taking a mental break to clear my mind by perusing the sunglasses store while considering grabbing a Hale & Hearty soup for lunch, a freaking bomb was being rolled into place just several hundred feet away and two stories below the soles of my shoes. The jihadis lit the twenty-minute fuse and scrambled out of the garage into the safety of daylight (they had no interest in being martyrs for Allah). Tick-tock.

I decided to make my way to the Citibank kiosks to get cash, which were located near the wide and steep escalators that led even deeper down to the PATH train station and underground parking. I was heading right toward Tower One when at precisely 12:17:37 p.m. I felt a shock wave of condensed air rip through me; it was as if someone had snuck up on me and boxed my ears and sucker punched me in the diaphragm in one swift motion. Then came the violent flickering of lights followed by the low muffled roar from two levels underground. The floor trembled.

I halted in my tracks and briefly stooped over to catch my breath. That was odd, I thought. My first thought was: a thunderstorm in February? Then came the high-pitched screams from a panicked crowd that was suddenly running toward me from the very direction I was headed as if a T. rex was on their tails. Something terrible had happened. I found myself facing a mob of hysterical pedestrians who were now stumbling past me almost knocking me down as they headed in abject panic for the exits up to Liberty Street. A rolling avalanche of smoke followed the stampede like some malevolent cloud from a horror novel. My second theory, once I'd wiped my mental grease board clean of the silly winter thunderstorm notion, was that some lunatic with an assault rifle was going apeshit down there just out of sight and was heading my way, even though I heard no telltale pops of gunfire. It didn't matter. Everyone was running from *something*, so I figured I'd best start hoofing it too. One likes to think that under duress and in the fog of war they'll rise to the occasion and be the reincarnation of Horatius or Audie Murphy bravely doing battle with the enemy. The reality is sometimes far more humbling and disappointing. Imagine my mindset. There's maybe a madman with a gun headed my way. The exit is straight down a corridor right in front of me, up the stairs, and out onto the streets of Manhattan and relative safety. But the simple fact is I was scared out of my wits and so, being the well-trained warrior that I was, what did I do? Naturally, I dove like Homer Simpson during Sideshow Bob's robbery of the Kwik-E-Mart into the sunglass store that had no rear exit and promptly crouched down in hiding...behind a *glass* display case. Had I covered my eyes and chanted, "You can't see me," it would've been no less effective a ruse. Nothing like being cool under fire.

Fortunately for my pathetic butt there was no crazed gunman, and I soon reclaimed my senses about me enough to slink out from behind the protection of a transparent glass counter and make my way back into the promenade and out onto Liberty Street. The bomb failed to do what Yousef intended, which was topple Tower One into Tower Two and inflict a horror show of death and destruction. But his handiwork did leave a 110-foot-wide-and-several-stories-deep crater smoldering in the obliterated lower levels of World Trade Center Tower One. There were also, tragically, six innocent people lying dead... six regular souls who probably woke up that morning thinking about their weekend plans with no idea that this day would be their last on earth.

Smoke poured out of the gaping wound and climbed up the elevator shafts and stairwells all the way to the top of the 1,300-foot skyscraper. Rumor had it that a PATH transformer blew. No one then was thinking of terrorism as the default as we do now. With the immediate danger passed I actually made my way to the elevator banks of 4 WTC and glibly ascended back up to the trading floor, ready to resume my workday. When I got back into the pits the chatter was that the floor was shaken so violently because Mark Fisher, one of the NYMEX's most successful traders, dropped his wallet.

It wasn't long, though, before 4 WTC and the trading floor itself started to fill with acrid smoke, and amidst the decreasing visibility and increased coughing we decided it might not be a bad idea to wrap it up and vamoose. One announcement came over the loudspeaker trying to calm our fears, but it had the opposite effect. Apparently, all the trading floor functions were in operation, the loudspeaker voice assured us, despite what appeared to be a small fire somewhere in the WTC complex. All that was not working due to the blasted water main way down at the base of the crater were the sprinklers. Hmm. Fire yes and water no? Time to punch out for the weekend. We made our crowded way down the dark and narrow stairwells now satu-rated in blinding smoke, and I said a silent thank you that we had at most nine floors to descend. I thought about the folks up on the top floors of the high towers and was happy I wasn't one of them. Their trip down was ten times more arduous, and they were terribly exposed and vulnerable. Had Tower One collapsed, the carnage would have been beyond imagination.

As we huffed our tortuously slow descent down the jammed stairwell in a building far too old for its modern purpose, the still-solvent Leonid posed a question that was on all our minds: "Can you imagine being in smoke and fire like this but way up in the clouds in One or Two?"

No, I couldn't. "Meh, but what are the odds of that?" I asked. Slim to none. We concurred it would be well worth the minuscule risk factor for the sweet views.

CHAPTER 13

"TAKE YOUR CHARTS AND SHOVE 'EM"

I STARTED OFF TRADING PRODUCT options inauspiciously losing money. I figured it was because I'd gone from a high liquidity/low volatility market to the exact opposite. It was the learning-curve phase. Before I knew it, though, I was down a hundred grand. I was growing despondent. Then a surprisingly patient Oscar once again taught me a valuable lesson. During his first trip to the FGT office since my arrival back in New York, we sat at a desk and went over my position. I was apologetic (I wasn't used to losing him money), but his tone was reassuring. "Don't worry about it," he advised me. "It's a growing pain that comes with a new trading environment. Just get out of your position, take the small loss, and start over from scratch with a fresh perspective." He was instructing me to lock in my losses (which is not an easy pill to swallow). Then I could trade going forward with a clear head. This risk-management exercise prompted me to examine my losers forensically. After that, I adopted a more nimble, less size-oriented approach to trading in the skittish energy markets. And, thanks to DAG's wise counsel, once I calmed down and adjusted my trading style, I began churning out steady profits in the heating oil/unleaded gas ring. Unfortunately, as events unfolded, I wouldn't always take Oscar's advice. Eventually I would fall prey to one of the most insidious predators of the successful trader: hubris. Once I started putting up positive returns again my head would swell and I'd end up defying him. Much to my detriment.

• • •

I've always had an eye for patterns, which goes back to my artist days. This eye got me into trouble with Oscar, and we would eventually part ways. I became fascinated with spread transactions. Basically, they are the simultaneous buying of one month while selling another. I noticed that the difference between April versus May in heating oil had widened significantly, meaning the April futures contract was trading for some reason at a steep premium to May delivery. This is called "backwardation" and it often occurs when there's fear of immediate scarcity in the product due to an unforeseen supply shortage. All else being equal, physical commodities spreads tend to trade in a manner where the nearer-term month is cheaper than further out in the same season. This is because supply further in the future is not guaranteed, and the cost that a buyer of any actual physical product would have to pay to store it for the extended time period is built into the proxy futures price. This "cost of carry" is reflected in more expensive corroborating futures contracts. Such markets where the near-term expiry is cheaper than further out is called a "normal" or "contango" configuration. I noticed that whenever the heating oil futures went backwardated, they would eventually move to tighten as the nearer-term contracts approached expiration until the two months traded at the same level. Such market action is called "convergence." I just happened to catch the activity on the charts that I religiously studied and divined this pattern from them.

In late March 1994, I saw that once again the nearest-term April heating oil contract was trading higher than the next month out May contract by over one full penny, or 100 ticks.[5] So, I decided to dip my toe in Oscar's forbidden speculative waters. I casually strolled from my spot in the product options over to the futures ring, shouted out a request for a market, and sold a few April/May heating oil spreads. Then the structure widened more to over 200 ticks. And I sold a few more. It widened more, so I sold again. And so on until I had a total position of short 400 April and long 400 May futures. This was a direct violation of the "never try and double-up to even-up" rule, and I was losing money on the trades. And yet, Roselyn and Oscar back in Chicago at first couldn't figure out why. As for every April contract I was short I was long a corresponding May, they just saw my overall futures position and it looked "flat" to them. Buying one thing and selling another is only truly "flat" if the buys and sales are contracts in the exact same months, meaning they have the same expiration. But I was, in fact, short the April/May spread and thus quite exposed as that spread could just continue to widen until April expired and my losses were locked in as I'd have to sell out the Mays at the much lower prices or suddenly be long four hundred naked heating oil futures when the Aprils went off the board. And I'd already

---

5   Each tick in heating oil and unleaded gasoline represented $0.0001 (.01 cents) per gallon and as each contract represented 42,000 gallons (same as 1,000 42-gallon bbl) each tick=$4.20.

seen with the Retail Sales nightmare what such exposure could do to an account.

Inevitably, Oscar did a deep dive into my positions and saw what I was up to. He called New York, fuming.

"I don't know what the hell you think you're doing, *Little Shafe*, but get out of your April/Mays and take the loss before it gets any worse," he growled over the speakerphone. "Then we need to have a long talk."

My legs weakened, but I tried to justify my rogue activity. "Oscar," I protested, "the charts tell me it'll come in."

"Let me tell you what I think about your fucking charts," he said. "In fact, take your charts and shove 'em. You're not a fund manager. *Get out of the spread.*"

"Okay."

But I didn't. In my mind, I wasn't being stubborn. I just knew I was right. But the spread kept widening to +$.045 or 450 ticks…and I kept selling until I was short five hundred April/Mays for an average of roughly $.03. Soon I was down almost $320,000. Alan was growing more anxious and, in fact, called Chicago without my knowing to express his concerns… as he should have, being the head of the New York office. My losses affected him too. It finally came to a head when he pulled me out of the mob and into the entrance leading to the trading floor. He then gave it to me straight. "Roselyn said if you don't exit this position first thing tomorrow then I have to do it."

Yet even as Alan issued this ultimatum, the spread started to give way and tighten. Over the course of the following day I did nothing, and the April/May started to tighten from +$.045 to +$.04 to +$.035…then +$.03…which was the price all my sales from +$.02 up to +$.04 had averaged into. My position went from being down $320,000 at its nadir to breakeven. I was excited. Yes, I'd defied Oscar, but I knew what I was doing. Just as I'd predicted, the spread continued moving my way—April was going lower and May was rebounding sharply higher as the prices were converging. I went to find Alan to let him know that now, since I was in the black, I was really going to let them have it and make a killing by *selling even more* April/Mays. I felt very much like a "big swinging dick" at that moment. I assured him I had every intention to buy my sales back when the spread got close to flat, even as I expected it to move con-tango. "I don't want to get greedy after all," I joked, so relieved I was almost in tears.

Instead of congratulating me on my intestinal fortitude and how my redemption would make everything right with Chicago, Alan handed me a set of trades showing him buying my five hundred April/May spreads at an average of +$.029. A ten-tick winner to be sure, but hardly the killing I was already tabulating in my head. For all my pain and sleepless nights I'd made a small profit of roughly $20,000 on my foray into specu-lative spread trading. Unbeknownst to me, as he'd told Chicago he would if I did nothing, Alan had put the order in through another broker. As I looked up at the board over the course of the long day I saw the April/May spread continue to contract: +$.025 then +$.012 and then even -$.005 the other way with April briefly trading under May. Traders were congratulating me on the "fortune" I must have made on those April/Mays and the brass ones it took for me to sell into 200 ticks against me. They had no idea the Great and Powerful Oscar in Chicago told Alan to get me out of the trade. I was beyond furious.

"What the fuck, Alan! Do you know how much coin you left on that table?"

But Alan was unapologetic. "Yes, I do. And you were right about this trade…this time." I went to say something, but he talked right over me. "Based on where it's trading now you probably would have made at least a six-hundred-grand profit. Maybe more. But what if you were wrong? What if something crazy in the markets that none of us down here in the boiler room knew about was going on? Something fundamental that none of us could see? What if the spread just kept moving wider and wider? Five hundred ticks. Six hundred? *A thousand?* What if you ended up losing a lot more than the three hundred grand you'd already given away?"

"That wasn't going to happen," I said rather prickly.

"Right," Alan replied, unmoved. "And Russia would never invade Afghanistan. And the Dow would never lose twenty-two percent in a day. And oil was definitely going to scream higher once the Gulf War started, right?" I had no retort to that. "I want you to imagine that phone call to Oscar when you tell him not only did you lose an enormous amount of his money, but you did it while *defying* him! Seriously, are you a complete idiot?"

That was the thing. It wouldn't have been the money per se, although no doubt for Oscar that would have hurt. It was that I violated two of his cardinal rules. 1) I treated my badge as a license to speculate rather than trade. 2) I defied him. He was the boss. And you do what the boss says or you move on. Period. I guarantee had I made him a small fortune he'd have still been in a rage because of how I did it. Speculation was just not what he was all about. I was in very deep, very hot water. (Although I have no doubt Oscar still would have taken the money.)

What I later realized, too, was that I'd succumbed to two of the worst enemies of the trader: greed and hubris. And in retrospect, I realize I was damned lucky. Alan was right. That spread could have very well kept widening... I have seen it do just that in the years since this episode. Although we made a tiny profit, Alan would have been just as right to buy the spreads back for a $300,000 loss. For several days the trade was steadily losing money. And as ZOF once declared, "When you lose it's not because the market goes against you. It's because you go against the market."

I'd made two other mistakes in putting on the trade, besides defying my boss and basically deceiving Chicago about the risk. I traded way too large for my account, and I didn't have a predetermined exit, or "uncle" point when I would have to admit I was wrong and get out. If you say to yourself, "I will sell this spread at +$.03, but if it trades above +$.045 I am out," then you decide how much you are willing to risk, and tailor your position size accordingly. It's Trading 101 really. If you sell 100 and give yourself a 10-point loss exit, it is no more or less risk than if you sell 10 and give yourself a 100-point loss exit. Either way, just make sure you have the discipline if you're wrong to pull the trigger and get out where you said you would when you entered the trade. A willingness to take a loss is an integral part of the business. It is inevitable. No one is right 100 percent of the time. The traders who survive are those who are unafraid to, and unfazed by, taking small losses. As Oscar was fond of saying, "I'm not a great trader. But I'm a great *puker!*"

Now, by sticking to your exit strategy you may find yourself getting out at the high or low of the market just before it turns back in your favor. There are very few aspects of trading as aggravating as that. You, in fact, feel like you've been played, or "shaken out" of your position, as the saying goes. Staring into your drink that night, you might be grumbling to yourself, "If I'd just held out a little longer…." But, amen I say to you, that one time you override your plan, say, "Screw my exit, I'm right, dammit!" and do nothing when your loss-exit point is reached, that will be the time when the trade will just keep going against you. And that's when a small loss can turn into a catastrophe. Live to fight another day. The market is like the ocean waves and you're a surfer. You can always catch the next one if this one passes you by.

A trader constantly has the demon of wanting ever more and more boring at all times. Especially when having a good run. As such, I often remind myself of Oscar's words of wisdom relevant not just to my escapades in supersized spread trading but every temptation to swing for the fence I've had to beat back over the course of my career. "Little Shafe," he once said in our more halcyon days, "I've made an awful lot of money by not trying to make an awful lot of money." It's whenever I deviate from this simple yet powerful mentality that I get in trouble.

So there I was, thanks to Alan's intervention, with twenty-one grand more in my account, but I'd lost Oscar's trust. And once lost, trust is a lot harder to get back than a losing month or two. Seeing my Wall Street adventures as paid grad school and knowing I would—and should—be fired for what I'd done, I tendered my resignation and eventually moved over to the American Stock Exchange to try my hand at trading equity options.

Although I became more interested in long-term trends than scalping ticks on the floor, it wasn't just the difference with

FGT management over trading strategy that prompted the rift. Things had changed in the firm. My brother and Max never quite recovered from the Retail Sales error. This had more to do with a disagreement with Oscar over how to allocate the loss than the money itself, creating a fissure of sorts. My brother and Max felt that had the error been $1 million in their favor that Oscar would have taken his 50 percent. So, it only stood to reason that an error of $1 million against them obliged Oscar to take half onto his books as well. Especially since it was the result of a clerical error. A clerk they never hired but were assigned. Oscar disagreed. "It was your fuckup. You own it." But I was in New York again by then and had no dog in the fight anymore. Max eventually left FGT as I did (albeit my days were numbered while his were not) to trade on his own while my brother left for Singapore.

Once set up on the AMEX, I ended up on that most obscure of the floor exchanges trading Philip Morris and then Intel options. But I never liked stock options trading. I especially didn't like the short selling rules put in place after the Crash of '87 that meant one could only go short a stock on an uptick. This meant that if a stock was trading at 50 having just traded at 50 1/16 you needed to wait for it to print 50 1/16 again or "uptick" before selling. If it went from 50 to 49 15/16 you still couldn't sell it. Nor could you if it then traded on another downtick to 49 7/8 then 49 13/16 and so on. Not until it went from maybe 49 13/16 back up to 49 7/8 could you sell it. This made options hedging tricky. Plus, I thought the specialist system was rigged. It reminded me more of Sicilian Cosa Nostra patronage than proper business. Also, I really didn't like dealing with fractions.[6]

I yearned to be back in commodities where it was about supply and demand more than false valuations and fudged earnings and insiders. Plus, I wanted to get off the trading floor. My ears had developed a more severe ring, and bad backs in the form of slipped discs and angry sciatic nerves ran in my family. After six years of screaming for a living, I decided it was time to move on. When I was on the NYMEX I often heard the firm Prebon floated around. It was a company involved in energy dealing in some capacity although I really wasn't sure how exactly. A former FGT clerk who was now trading natural gas with an outfit in Tulsa knew the heads of a new natural gas group at Prebon. They were an OTC group based in New Jersey. I was nearing thirty and married now. Trading profits came but also went. I thought it was time to grow up a little and leave the floor hijinks behind for a more steady income and a more stable lifestyle.

The trading pits could both exhilarate and age a man. Like a roller coaster that you suspected might just have a few tracks with rusted screws that could break off the trusses at any moment and send you hurtling to the ground. It had been a great experience, one I wouldn't trade for the world. But it was time to move on and exchange my aloha shirt, cheesy tie, and smock for a pin-striped suit, cufflinks, and wingtips. And so I did.

---

6   US stock exchanges eventually converted to decimals starting in August 2000 and completed the switch by April 2001.

CHAPTER 14

9/11 IN BRIEF

One perfectly gorgeous late-summer morning, I'd been working as a natural gas broker for Prebon in Jersey City for four years. I was no longer a trader, wherein I took the principal risk for my own account. I was now an OTC broker. Specifically natural gas derivatives. This was the "upstairs" equivalent of RKR and WULF. But in the OTC world, it was the traders for the banks and big marketing firms and utilities who had the power, as they dispensed their orders to the brokers they liked the most. It was not skill or market knowledge that drove success as a broker, but rather personality and, of course, how much you entertained those on the other end of the phone. Some of my customers began as purely professional relationships, but eventually morphed into great friends with whom I would go out to dinner or junkets on a regular basis. Others I had never even met. They were just a voice on the other end of the phone, calling in from another city or, later as the technology advanced, an Instant Messenger ID and line of text.

If you were lucky, you befriended a trader who slung so much wood, and thus fed you so many commission dollars, it was like printing money. One broker had somehow become BFFs with a trader for a hedge fund who moved tens of thousands of natural gas options contracts each day like clockwork. Once, when attempting to actually expand his client book beyond that one trader at one shop—whose sudden death or departure from the business would abruptly end the broker's gravy train, and career—he literally turned to me in the middle of a cold call, palmed the phone's speaker, and asked, "Hey, what do we broker?" The professional broker literally had no idea what the derivatives he was even moving were! But it didn't matter, as his only customer paid him millions in commissions per year. A smart trader like Oscar will make exponentially more than a smart broker like FOZ. But a dimwitted broker, so long as he has the right friends to support him, will make a lot more than a similarly dull trader. By moving off the floor I was back in the familiar position where who I knew mattered more than what I knew.

Brokering OTC came with its own stresses as your future wasn't so much in your own hands as those of the guys on the other ends of the phones. And if the day was slow, unlike the floor, it was up to you to make something happen. Maybe you'd make up an options structure and throw it out into the market to see if there were any bites. And you were always on the phone trying to whip up business with your clients. We called it "dialing for dollars."

And yet, even "upstairs" off the trading floor, within the more subdued environment of business suits, desks with family photos, blinking phone banks, and spreads of PC monitors, the impulse to have fun at others' expense was pervasive. My favorite gag was the one we played on the brokers who came into the office with packed travel bags. They would have a flight to catch out of Newark in the afternoon and so they would bring their luggage in with them. We would wait until they stepped off the desk and then quickly grab the heaviest books on the shelves, preferably the *Stalsby Energy Directory*, which listed the names, addresses, and contacts of every energy company in North America. But any book with any heft to it would do. Dictionaries, textbooks, Russian novels, anything like that. Then we'd open the mark's luggage and stuff the books in among his clothing and other wares and zip the bags back up. When the broker left the office to catch his car service to the airport, he found himself inexplicably struggling to hoist bags that weighed as much as sacks of bricks...which he in effect was unknowingly toting around. Only later on, when he arrived in his hotel room with sore shoulders and strained biceps and unpacked his bags, did we get the texts calling us "assholes" and threatening vengeance. Some things never change.

• • •

By September 11, 2001, I'd seen a lot of interesting things in my life. Manhattan right across the Hudson River was never dull. But nothing could prepare me for the horrors we all witnessed that day. We stood on the twenty-fourth floor of a skyscraper on the western bank of the river, watching helplessly as the North Tower burned furiously as the result of what we heard was an aircraft impact. As a historian of sorts, this didn't shock me since I knew that in 1945 a twin-engine B-25 Mitchell medium bomber had slammed into the seventy-ninth floor of the Empire State Building, killing fourteen, so that was always a risk when constructing high rises in the same airspace as three major commercial airports and a smattering of smaller fields...

although I thought this accident strange as the bomber had been disoriented by a thick fog, whereas on this morning the air was cloudless and crisp with unlimited visibility. As we watched the spreading fire from our high windows, we suddenly heard the whining of a jetliner as United Airlines Flight 175 ominously appeared overhead and made an erratic U-turn over the waters south of lower Manhattan. The 767 then gunned the engines and slammed on an angle into the seventy-eighth to eighty-fourth floors of World Trade Center Two, the South Tower. We knew we were watching something sinister and devastating unfold and, like the rest of the country, tried to make sense of it all in the shock and horror that followed. As dealers it was natural for us to wonder what this meant for the markets. As it turned out, it meant very little.

For all its horror and the shockwave it sent around the globe, 9/11 had no real effect on energy prices considering the immensity of the event. The average level of front-month crude oil for Q4 2001 was actually $7.50/bbl lower than it had been in Q3 2001 when the attacks took place. The lessons of the Gulf War were well learned by now, and no one was panic buying. The same nonimpact of the terror attacks occurred in natural gas with prices fluctuating lazily between the lows of just above $2.00/mmbtu[7] in September 2001 to just below $2.50 by year's end. Ours was a domestically produced commodity and as our business was, in the end, about supply and demand neither was significantly affected by the events of that awful day. The gas continued to flow as the Henry Hub, the main station for

---

7   mmbtu=one million British thermal units, the standard size for a Natural Gas futures contract

natural gas distribution on the Gulf of Mexico, was obviously not in any conflict zone. As much as the nation felt 9/11 on a visceral level, from an antiseptic trading perspective the attacks were four isolated events that would not impact demand for energy in any way, as might a widespread natural disaster or some other more crippling terrorist attack involving a nuclear, biological, or cyber strike, or an assault on the nation's electric grid such as a solar flare.

So the consequences of that day were more of a personal than business nature. As a precaution, considering we had no idea if more planes were en route, we evacuated the building (although a few of us doubted that an obscure skyscraper in Jersey City was on any target list). People spilled out into the streets under the bright sunshine and migrated to the pier that jutted out like a stiff appendage into the lapping waters of the Hudson. The imagery was surreally apocalyptic as the two tallest buildings in the city, and second in height nationally only to Chicago's Sears Tower, were engulfed in flames like two gargantuan Roman candles. We could see this was something well beyond the scope of any fire department as the thick oily black smoke belched and roared into the air oddly contrasted against the backdrop of an otherwise perfectly clear azure sky.

We all knew people up in those towering infernos as many Wall Street firms were housed in them. A very well-liked Prebon lawyer had said his tearful goodbyes to us barely a month before. He would miss us all but was excited by the opportunities his new position as counsel for Cantor Fitzgerald offered him, so we of course wished him Godspeed. And now he was trapped up there on the 101st floor as a fire so intense it was melting steel raged below him and presented him and others with the diabolical choice of either staying where he was and roasting alive or leaping over a thousand feet to his death. I hope he was unconscious from the smoke before he ever had to face such a choose-your-poison moment. He was one of eight residents of my New Jersey commuter town to lose their lives, including my neighbor's son, still in his early twenties. They were among the 658 Cantor employees to die that day. That was two-thirds of their entire staff, including the brother of their CEO, Howard Lutnick; Howard was spared the same fate because he was late for work, having first sent his kid off to the first day of school.

As the fires grew more intense, the gravity of what was happening sank in even before the towers buckled and collapsed, one then the other, and people all around me began to cry and moan. One broker standing next to me was in tears. I asked him blankly if he was okay. He looked at me with forlorn shock. "My two brothers are up there." They too worked for Cantor Fitzgerald. They both died.

You know the rest about that day.

But what I don't think many outside our industry know was just how much we pulled together as a professional community in the aftermath. Prebon had two competitors who'd both had their flagship offices in the Twin Towers: Cantor Fitzgerald and Euro Brokers, which was up on the eighty-fourth floor of Tower Two and lost sixty-one people. In an act of compassion and decency that gave me renewed faith in a business that seemed hell-bent at times on driving even the most optimistic into the land of the cynic, our management opened up our dealing floor to the survivors. Our phones were their phones. Our desks were their desks. Most brokerage and trading floors have empty desks either in anticipation of expansion or due to the shutting down of divisions. While our competitors moved to pick up the pieces and recover (and mourn their dead) the office saw many a strange face in the hallways or on the desks. And that was just fine by us. Humanity does thrive on Wall Street. For a little while, anyway.

CHAPTER 15

THE BIG DOG AND THE FOX

THE PROBLEM WITH MOVING MONEY for a living, whether on a raucous trading floor or a more subdued high-rise office in which I'd found myself at Prebon, is that you do not make anything tangible. You have no product, no patents, no brand. In short, every night a company's "assets" take the elevator to the lobby. As with floor trading, the world of OTC dealing in energy was populated by so many freaks and oddballs that the business could make the Mos Eisley Cantina in *Star Wars* look like an IBM convention. Managing such a crew is a daunting task. But at some point, one looks at management and asks what they have to offer besides a phone and desk that could possibly justify giving them fifty cents on the dollar of every commission you book or profit you earn. Eventually I grew tired of working for others. And so I tried my hand at starting my own brokerage company.

The seas over which my little boutique concern sailed were never calm. Storms could erupt from otherwise clear blue skies and take their psychological toll on me. In recruiting brokers to join my fledgling enterprise I had to convince people that my partner Danny, who had been an excellent Prebon broker in his day before taking a leave of absence for drug rehab, was clean and sober. Danny may have been at the time, but several of those who joined the firm were not. In fact, drug use right under my very nose was severe...but in this respect I was too naïve to understand it. I'd done my share of drinking and casual drugs as business required. And cocaine was so pervasive on the floor of the CME that one had to be careful it was only sugar he was putting in his coffee. But never had I seen the hard stuff that made a comeback of sorts in the caverns of Wall Street. Heroin and Oxycontin were the culprits.

On Wall Street, where there is youth and money and alpha males, there will be drugs...and my own firm was far from immune. The dilemma I faced as an OTC brokerage business owner was this: if I fired everyone doing drugs I would have had few producers left. One thing that the real business world shows is that there is a myriad of management problems that MBA classes simply cannot fathom. For instance, what do you do if in the middle of the day one of your top producers gets up and leaves the office ostensibly to "grab a quick bite"... *and never comes back*? This happened to us. His whereabouts were a mystery for a full twelve hours until I got a phone call at home from his girlfriend informing me that he'd checked himself into a drug rehab clinic upstate and would not be coming back. How do you explain that one to customers? The answer is in a straightforward and professional manner. You simply say that their broker has had to take a sabbatical for "personal reasons," but you cannot by law say any more about it at this time (whether true or not). "But if you're free for dinner I can fill you in." Maybe you'd even get a new customer out of it. Life goes on.

• • •

The company Danny and I co-founded with a third investor would balloon to twenty-three employees at its peak. That rapid growth was due to having launched the firm in late 2005; the timing couldn't have been more propitious. It was the same period in which the epic cage match between the two largest OTC energy traders was coming to a boil. In one corner was a former Enron money machine, John Arnold. At just thirty-two years old, the soft-spoken Texan was now running his own Centaurus hedge fund from an office high above Houston's posh Galleria. In the other was the Canadian upstart Brian Hunter, trading natural gas for the fund Amaranth out of either his Calgary or Greenwich location.

A blow-by-blow account of Hunter's rise and fall as one of the most consequential natural gas traders in history can be found in abundance in the financial literature. Stories of his stint trading for Deutsche Bank where he made healthy profits for their natural gas team are legion. That was until he stubbornly held on to a losing short position into a spell of unexpected and severe cold weather that sent prices higher in the last two months of 2003 and gave back over $50 million, effectively wiping out his year. It wasn't the losses so much as the willingness of Hunter to take enormous leveraged risk and disregard instructions to pare down his exposure that concerned his managers. In a way, he was like me with my April/Mays, but with exponentially more money at stake. And, like me with FGT, once that happened his days at the bank were numbered.

Unlike me, Hunter was offered hefty signing bonuses by several hedge funds inviting him to take his expertise to their shops (one reportedly in seven figures). In the end, he opted to join a firm that would, it turned out, give him the most rope with which to hang himself. For one year, beginning with Hurricane Katrina in August 2005, it seemed that Amaranth had made a smart move in bringing him on. He'd gone long ungodly volumes of natural gas futures and bullish options strategies before the Category 5 storm slammed into the Gulf of Mexico, causing over $125 billion in damage and severely curtailing energy production for months. Natural gas futures soared to as high as $15.78/mmbtu in the January 2006 contract—more than double the $7.00/mmbtu levels at the beginning of the year. It's estimated Hunter's positions made north of a billion dollars, earning the Canadian *wunderkind* a nine-figure bonus before his thirty-first birthday. Meanwhile down in the Big Easy they were mourning 1,800 fatalities. As with the Gulf War, others' pain was the trading community's gain.

But by spring the following year Hunter's wings were already starting to melt under the searing sunlight of a sense of invincibility, the classic "I *am* the market!" syndrome. Ego boosts from the cadre of sycophantic brokers that latched onto him like pilot fish—catering to his every whim while showering him with gifts, the hottest tickets, and paid-for junkets to exotic locales—certainly added to his sense of his own divinity. Perhaps he just suffered from the same affliction that infected the triumphant Lee before Gettysburg or Yamamoto before Midway...a dangerous overconfidence that military historians call "victory disease." Whatever his condition, such a sudden and hefty income can change a man. In her book *Hedge Hogs*, Barbara T. Dreyfuss's definitive account of Amaranth's demise, and that of its master-of-the-universe trader, she mentions that former coworkers from Hunter's modest days at his first employer TransCanada who ran into him a few years later noticed he "now had more of a taste for $400 bottles of wine than $40 bottles."

Although 2006 began spectacularly for him—from January to April Hunter had made Amaranth $1.67 billion trading—the warning signs were all there. After returning 12 percent in April, Hunter saw his enormous position bleed $1.1 billion in May alone. Such a massive P&L swing should have told him to reduce his trading size before something really bad happened. But instead of paring down his position, Hunter added to his bets in natural gas options and futures strategies that would benefit from a cool summer followed by a severe hurricane season and then a subsequently cold winter. None of these forecasts panned out. By August 2006, Hunter, who by now had certainly earned the title he so craved as the biggest swinging dick in natural gas by volume (sometimes being responsible for over half the daily trading activity in certain contract months), was in trouble.

I didn't care about the peril Amaranth investors were in, per se. After May 2006's ten-figure hit, management should have seen their star trader was dancing with the fund's entire existence on a knife's edge of risk. When in one month a trader's account is literally up one billion and the next down a billion and then the next up a billion again and so on as Hunter's P&L was behaving into the summer of 2006—out of a total of just $9.6 billion under management in the entire fund—it's a pretty good clue that said trader is out of control and all risk management protocols have broken down. One day he was going to lose big... and just keep losing.

Some Amaranth investors did, in fact, see the handwriting on the wall and pull their money out. The huge investment firm BlackRock, for example, ate the 3 percent early withdrawal penalty after concluding Amaranth's management had lost all control over their demigod trader and that any so-called risk monitoring would prove totally inadequate when the rubber of Amaranth's fatally flawed stress testing VAR model hit the reality of the real market action road.[8]

What mattered to me and my new energy brokering company during all this was that enormous trades were going down and, even if we didn't do business for Hunter directly, the effects of his trading in 2006 blew through the market like shrapnel and hit all of us. If, for example, he took down ten thousand options over there, then those counterparties he just traded with might have to do something over here to offset the risk. And we got much of that runoff. We didn't make tens of millions as the lucky few in Hunter's dog pound did, but we did make a good living, and I was content.

The positions Hunter was accumulating were based on his belief, or rather hope, that 2006 would be another severe hurricane season. He was also putting on enormous positions in a spread wherein he was long March and short April natural gas futures. A cold winter would prompt the market to buy the winter (March) more aggressively than the spring (April), earning him an enormous profit. But neither the hurricane sea-

---

8   VAR=value-at-risk. It is a theoretical assessment of a position's exposure to various potential price action scenarios. Amaranth's model showed Hunter's exposure to unfavorable market moves to be a roughly $350 million VAR. This was a disastrously flawed analysis. Hunter's true VAR, as events would show, was in the many billions.

son of 2006 nor the winter of 2007 would amount to anything. Furthermore, he'd made a bet that the summer of 2006 would be mild temperature-wise and shorted futures. Instead, an unexpected heat wave descended over the entire country like melted brass. Temperatures from coast to coast soared. The mercury in Fargo, North Dakota, registered one hundred degrees, breaking a record that had stood since 1929. So Hunter found himself short summer (into a heat wave) long hurricane months (into a tame season) and long a cold winter (into a balmy forecast). His positions were bleeding money. And, as he'd positioned himself to be *the* market, he was now married to them. And everyone in the natural gas market, even the floor rats, who were usually the last to know (hence Oscar's heated admonitions against speculating from down in the pits) knew he was trapped in a snare of his own invention.

I try to imagine what was going through Hunter's head when he fired up his BlackBerry while on a broker-sponsored boondoggle and saw that in one day alone the enormous positions he'd been unable to even try to defend (not that he could have anyway) while out on the links and incommunicado had cost his firm $650 million… a figure that made our Retail Sales number look like a rounding error. Apparently, he wasn't bothered by it in the least. That night he and his brokers (and their wives) ate dinner, slurped expensive wines, and laughed it up as if he hadn't a care in the world. And really, as far as Hunter was concerned, he didn't. With a net worth of over $150 million by this point while still several years short of thirty-five, what did it matter if he lost billions for the fund that had so loved him when he was making them big profits by rolling a pair of cinder block–sized dice? It wasn't *his* money after all. And besides, he'd already won the lottery trading Hurricane Katrina the year before when his strategies that were today destroying Amaranth yielded ten-figure profits.

Even if Hunter ended up having to give back maybe $50 million either in CFTC fines over manipulative trading practices or whatever restitution the investors concocted and the lawyers demanded he cough up to make them go away, there really wasn't much of a lifestyle change to go from having $150 million in the bank to $100 million when he preferred to live in Calgary where USD $3 million would buy him a custom-built dream house overlooking a breathtakingly scenic Rocky Mountain valley. Life would always be good for him. Later, one of the dealers who'd broken bread with him one evening as Hunter occasionally glanced down without expression to his BlackBerry said: "You'd never know the guy'd just taken what we thought at the time was a billion-dollar hit in one day. It didn't faze him."

Disgruntled former Amaranth coworkers told of Hunter and his loyal band of subordinate traders cracking jokes and casually tossing a football around the office during the week he took down the entire hedge fund—including any bonuses the other traders with families and not already worth $150 million had worked so hard to earn. I guess there was no fiddle for him to play, so the football sufficed. Although, to be fair to Hunter, these same fuming traders benefitted when the Big Dog's part of the energy group raked in enormous profits to attract gobs of investment capital into their employer's war chest, which directly benefitted their own W2s as they could trade larger and thus earn more income for themselves. After all, as H. I.

McDunnough points out in *Raising Arizona,* "There ain't no pancake so thin it don't got two sides."

But traders have short memories. Except for when they lose their jobs. And that was what happened when Hunter's overleveraged positions inevitably went pear-shaped, and one of the epic disasters in the annals of modern finance went down.

• • •

You have to work pretty hard to lose almost $7 billion in a week. Hunter managed to do just that. Although he was coldly indifferent to the devastation his activities had wrought, it was an agonizing experience for Amaranth's remaining investors, such as county pension funds representing teachers and public servants and others far removed in both geography and understanding of what was happening to their quickly evaporating money. But, once again, as seems to be the mantra of the trading and brokering business, their pain was our gain. The day after Hunter flew back from a golf outing, for example, the hosting broker received a call calmly instructing him to sell tens of thousands of one-year-out strips of call options. And these phone calls and instant messages from Hunter and his assistants were going out all over the broker community. One broker was paid a million dollars in fees for one day's work…somehow, even though the fund lost billions, they managed to scrape together the money to pay the commissions.

As lucrative as it was to be a broker in the Big Dog's pound, being one of the traders on the other side of Hunter's epic collapse was a far better deal…if you had the deep pockets and diamond-hard testicles to stay the course in the face of his attempts to artificially squeeze you out of your fundamentally correct position in natural gas spreads and other derivatives by relentlessly buying and pushing the market up in your face until you were compelled by margin calls to turn the paper loss into a real one. This happened to one well-respected fund manager who got the trade right but entered just a little too big and a tad too early to withstand the paper losses he was incurring due to Hunter's Banzai charge of nonstop buying, especially of the March/April spread, known in energy trading circles as "the widow-maker" for its propensity to gyrate wildly with the slightest weather events. Eventually the fund manager's investors couldn't take the heat and bailed on him, forcing him to buy back his shorts and lock in his losses in a liquidation to meet a wave of redemptions.

Down in Houston, John Arnold was also taking heavy paper losses as Hunter dug his own grave deeper and deeper by buying gas that no one with any fundamental understanding of the supply/demand dynamic in play would want anywhere close to these inflated prices once he stopped his artificial short squeeze. But Arnold had made his investors a mint already, and they'd learned to trust his judgment. So the ever-calm trader patiently waited for Hunter's inevitable tumble from the mountaintop once he ran out of bullets and had to turn around and offload his position…to no one. When Amaranth initiated a fire sale of their non-energy positions just to meet Hunter's rising margin calls, The Street knew there was blood in the water.

The besieged Canadian's problems only worsened when on August 29, 2006, the expiration day of the September 2006 contract, he decided to make a huge play by selling more of the September futures and buying the October throughout the course of the day. Since he owned the more expensive leg, he was effectively long the September/October spread starting at 36 ticks October over. By noon, his selling of September and buying of October had pushed the spread to as wide as October trading 50 over September...meaning what Hunter was short (September) was falling more than what he was long (October). The trade was moving in his favor. Or, more correctly, he was muscling it his way.

Given the sheer size Hunter was trading, he inevitably widened the differential between the two months, which in turn prompted him to pay higher and higher prices to keep it moving in his favor. He was caught in a vicious cycle. Still, he figured that, as the September contract would expire in a few hours, he might just run out the clock before any correction occurred. By 1:30 p.m. that afternoon, the September futures had only one hour left until it expired and so its settlement price would be locked in place. Hunter could then sell out his long October position, which wasn't set to expire for another month, and be flat, with a tidy profit. All would be well...at least for this day.

That's when Arnold made his move. He sensed from the sudden slowing of trading activity that Hunter had run out of ammo and thus was no longer able to hold his September shorts down relative to the long Octobers to protect his massive bet. This was due to trading limits and the already enormous size of his other positions relative to his total capital. (In some months Amaranth held over half of the total amount of open interest[9] on the exchanges.)

---

9   The number of contracts or commitments outstanding in futures and options that are trading on an official exchange at any one time.

Arnold, however, had a deeper reservoir of money, along with a fundamental conviction, based on both weather forecasts and gas in storage going into the end of summer, that the spread should be closer to flat than October trading a full fifty cents over September. So once Hunter was done, with less than an hour to go before the contracts expired, Arnold swooped in and bought thousands of September futures…the very ones Hunter was short and needed to stay low into expiry. His quiver now empty, the Big Dog could only watch helplessly as his enemy—for he saw Arnold as his chief rival—pushed up the September contract in his face with a torrent of unrelenting buying. By the time the clock hit 2:30 p.m. and the September contract's final settlement was posted, the spread, which had shown Hunter a hefty profit when it was trading at $0.50 to the October just forty-five minutes before, settled at a mere six cents. Arnold had crushed him.

This one episode cost Amaranth another $600 million. Hunter fumed, insisting that he was the victim of market manipulation. But no. He was just on the losing end of a battle he initiated. In short, his ego was now writing checks his dwindling account could no longer cash. The market knew that he was in a bind. And they had no interest in letting him out without a serious, even fatal, exit toll.

Finally, inevitably, with the March/April spread steadily collapsing in the face of a serene winter outlook, once again earning its ominous "widow-maker" sobriquet, with his losses in other overleveraged positions across the board mounting, it was time for Hunter to shut it all down and pay the piper. But his inventory of futures and options was so colossal that there was no way he could ever trade out of them piecemeal. The market would eat him alive. As such, Hunter's last hope to offload his enormous portfolio that stretched out for years along the curve was to find someone willing to buy the entire decimated book in one trade. It was the only way Amaranth could raise the funds quickly enough to meet its multi-billion-dollar margin calls from anxious clearing firms. In desperation, Hunter went directly to the victorious Arnold—whose inventory of futures and options was the opposite of the defeated Canadian's now-hemorrhaging natural gas book—and asked him to name a price to take it all off his hands. The bid Arnold showed was both reasonable and devastating. The taciturn Texan was telling Hunter in no uncertain terms that without his artificially moving the market where he wanted it to go, *this* was the true value of his depleted book. Take it or leave it. Hunter left it.

As it turned out, another hedge fund, Citadel, and the energy trading group at J.P. Morgan took Amaranth's losing positions onto their books for a slightly better price than Arnold had shown, if still at a crushing discount. The giant one-off transaction stopped the bleeding. But Amaranth, the once admired hedge fund whom their rogue trader had brought to its knees, was forced to shut its doors for good. There were at least no market repercussions as it was an orderly and contained unwind.

When the hedge fund/IB duo made its final price for buying what remained of Hunter's demolished position to close out his trades in one massive asset transfer, the losing trader chafed at the great "deal" the buyers were getting at his expense. "Brian was right; it was a good deal for us," said my Citadel client, who was one of the hedge fund's chief traders assigned to take the book onto their balance sheet. But he reminded Hunter that "maybe you shouldn't put yourself in a position to hold a fire sale to begin with."

After grudgingly accepting the terms of the position transfer—thus locking in what was at the time the largest loss suffered by any single trader in Wall Street history—Hunter asked the Citadel trader with a hint of irritation at surrendering his massive portfolio that had defined him for two years: "You sure you can handle a book this size?" My customer, a math whiz, and as humbly brilliant as the man chafing on the other end of the phone was patronizing, was honest. "No," he said, "I'll just have to do my best." And though he was above ever pointing it out, the irony of the question considering who'd asked it was self-evidently astounding. It certainly showed that even at the very end, after he'd destroyed a business that others worked years to build, and sent investors across the country reeling, he never lost his sense of who he was…the biggest monster trader to ever sling natural gas. He also was finished in the industry.

As for John Arnold, who'd won the game of high-stakes chicken, Reuters reported that in 2006 his fund returned over 300 percent net of fees. He's retired now and doing charitable work with his Matterhorn-sized pile of money. Well played.

Interesting side note. Although Hunter's 2006 losses eclipsed the $4.6 billion lost by bond-trading guru John Meriweather's hedge fund Long-Term Capital Management (LTCM) in 1998, which had been the most sizeable nonfraud-related trading loss in history up to that point, astoundingly just two years later, the Big Dog himself would be dethroned as trading's single biggest losing individual. This accomplishment was courtesy of a relatively unknown credit default swaps trader at the staid white shoe investment bank Morgan Stanley. Howie Hubler managed to sacrifice an astounding $9 billion to the gods of the market, albeit real quiet-like. To my knowledge, all of these men who had, as the phrase went, "blown up their books" managed to walk away from their debacles with tens of millions. Wall Street is one of the only businesses wherein over the course of your career you can be a net loser and still come out on top. I liken it to an architect who may have designed a house or two that stayed up nicely but then designed a skyscraper that came crashing down and still walked away from the rubble with millions. Nice work if you can get it.

CHAPTER 16

"GET IN THERE AND TRADE!"

THERE'S STILL ONE STORY I need to wind up here. Remember poor Jim Barkhorn? Trader JEB whom we left hanging back on October 20, 1987, as he stood weak-kneed in the Eurodollar options pit facing financial ruin the moment the futures began trading over 150 ticks higher than where they'd settled the day before?

At 7:20 a.m. the bell on the floor of the Chicago Merc dinged and there was an explosion of screams in the large Eurodollar futures pit. But in the adjacent options pit there was nothing but a subdued silence on the parts of the stunned traders. No one could believe what they were hearing. The futures, for which a 25-tick higher or lower open was unheard-of, were trading *250 higher*! The options brokers lining the top step from ZOF to WULF to RKR and the rest were frantically shouting down to the traders to make markets for their clerks to flash to the yellowcoats on the phones with funds and banks all over the world. But no one was really sure how to value anything against futures that had just opened a stupefying 250 ticks higher than the previous close. It seemed far too risky to even try. (Remember, each tick equaled $25, and usually the smallest trading size in the options was a hundred cars.)

One gruff broker, RIZ (whom one trader described as a cross between Danny DeVito and Charles Manson), was growing desperate and demanded a price on an option. He didn't care what level. He needed to show something, anything, to his anxious customers. He berated the shell-shocked crowd down in the pit below him. "December forty-five calls! Goddammit, you lazy pussies! Do your fucking jobs and show me something! *Anything!*" Silence still. The traders were all just staring at the futures market.

Finally, while the stunned Barkhorn stood motionless, contemplating losing his entire net worth, the experienced and calculating Bill Gladstone standing next to him saw an opportunity. Given the levels that he could hear trading in the nearby futures pit, against which the options were priced, GATS quickly spun the math in his head. He figured the option was worth something around 150 ticks and so he broke the stillness and shouted: "Fuck it! One hundred at two hundred! Hundred-up!" JEB was at first amazed at the brazenness of GATS for making a 100-tick-wide market…this was in a pit in which 3-tick-wide markets were howled down as ludicrously wide. But not today. All bets were off.

Instead of reading Gladstone the riot act for such an insultingly wide bid/offer, RIZ shouted, "Buy one hundred!" For his part, rather than look shocked, the confident GATS barked with joy! He'd just made six figures on his first trade. "Anyone *else?*" the broker pleaded. Sensing the young Barkhorn was in a fog, GATS grabbed him by the shoulders and said, "Jim! You've already lost all you had! That's gone! So you may as well go down swinging. But trust me; this day's going to make you! Snap out of it! Get in there and trade! *Trade!*"

JEB pulled himself out of his stupor and put his hand up. "Sell you a hundred!"

"Buy 'em!" screamed the grateful broker, knowing full well how much money he was giving away. Soon the other traders began to shout, "Sold! Sold!" as well. It quickly became apparent to Jim Barkhorn, thanks to the counsel of the kindly Bill Gladstone, that what he thought would be his last day on the floor had the potential to be a gold mine. Jim embarked on a frenzy of making markets. Soon he was trading at a furious pace. Throughout the day, as the markets gyrated wildly, JEB's cards filled with hastily scribbled transactions. By 2:00 p.m., when the closing bell sounded the end of the craziest trading day ever seen in the usually staid Eurodollar pits, Jim had overwhelmed his clerk, Mitch, with stacks of hastily filled out trading cards.

Then came the moment of reckoning. As the floor cleared out and his adrenaline subsided, the full reality of what the day might portend hit him. *I could be bankrupt*, JEB thought to himself. What was he going to tell his wife? How could he face his family? Mitch, his yellow smock streaked with ink strokes and stained with sweat, walked over to him with a sheet of paper and calculator in his hand.

"How bad is it?" said JEB, dreading the final P&L tally his clerk was about to relay to him.

"Well," said Mitch, "I have you losing around three hundred thousand on the open."

Jim's stomach flipped. That was actually more than had been in his account that morning. He was not only ruined, but now he was also in debt to his FCM. Images of his wife and young children in a homeless shelter as the Chicago winter approached while he worked odd jobs to pay off his six-figure margin call flashed through his mind. But he pushed them away and tried to remain composed. "I figured. I'm sorry, Mitch. I never expected the market to ever do what it did today."

"Why are you apologizing?" Mitch replied earnestly.

"I guess you won't be working for me anymore."

"Are you firing me?" his clerk asked.

"What? No. But, I mean, I'm broke now. I won't need a clerk when they escort me off the floor, will I?"

Mitch smiled, understanding Jim's concern. "You didn't let me finish. Yeah, you lost three hundred in your position, but you made just over a million trading. You're up around seven hundred fifty grand on the day."

Barkhorn's legs turned to rope, and he had to sit down on one of the cluttered steps in the pit. "Mitch, please tell me you're not messing with me."

The clerk bent over and handed JEB his final P&L with a broad grin. "I triple-checked my math and even confirmed it with the FCM. Congratulations, Boss."

The yellowcoat then moved on to his other charges. As the floor emptied, Jim remained seated. He glanced around at the near-vacant pit, with its layer of torn papers, abandoned trading cards, gum wrappers, newspapers, crushed Tic Tac boxes, and other bits of debris from this day of days and didn't know whether to shout for joy or cry with relief.

"See? You did all right today, didn't you?" It was a familiar, comforting voice. Jim turned around to see GATS grinning down at him from the top step. "You know what they say. When people get greedy, it's time to panic. But when people panic, boy is it time to get greedy. And they sure panicked today. Come on. Buy you a drink."

"In a few minutes," JEB said. He was still taking it all in.

"Merc Club. Fifteen minutes. Be there. You have a lot to celebrate."

GATS disappeared over the rim of the top step. Jim looked up at the boards showing the final prices that confirmed it had been the most volatile trading day since the Eurodollar contract was first listed on the floor in 1981. He put his head in his hands and rocked back and forth while still seated in the options pit wherein he'd done so much today. Then JEB began to sob. And he didn't care who saw him.

Jim Barkhorn would go on to be one of the most profitable traders on the floor, earning millions over the next few years. He would eventually partner with Bill Gladstone and then expand their firm until they became one of the most successful groups on the floor. A true man of faith, and believing he'd been spared financial ruin to pursue a higher calling than merely piling up more money than his modest tastes could ever require, Barkhorn would leave the business several years later, at the height of his financial prowess, to spread his wealth by founding Christian mission stations across the world. He was eternally grateful to God for the second chance October 20, 1987, gave him. That is the one thing the Almighty and the trading pits have in common. "The Lord giveth, and the Lord taketh away." Fortunately for JEB, in his case, the order was reversed. And so he survived to fight another day.

CHAPTER 17

A GREAT RUN

By 2007, I'd been an OTC natural gas broker longer than I'd been a trader. My days crammed chest-to-back amidst the screams, yells, and deafening noise of the mosh pit seemed another life ago. So more for nostalgia than any real business purpose, I decided to visit the new NYMEX exchange floor located in One North End Avenue. This was a modern fifteen-story building situated next to Brookfield Place along the eastern bank of the Hudson River. It was just a few blocks north of the giant footprints of the destroyed Twin Towers, now a museum/memorial, and a vast improvement from the depressing cave in which I'd worked at the demolished 4 World Trade.

The traders were standing around, whiling away the hours in their new space-age arena. As a testament to its growing importance as an energy source, the natural gas pit had a prominently positioned ring that in size almost matched that of the exchange's flagship crude oil pit. There were a few familiar faces, but most of the traders were strangers to me. I stood on the periphery by a phone bank and soaked in the atmosphere, what little there was. The old vibrancy had drained from this place. The heady days of the Gulf War were a thing of the distant past. I noticed the traders didn't carry paper pricing sheets anymore. Now they worked through electronic tablets resting on their forearms with stylus pens in hand. On these devices, they managed their positions, received real-time P&L and margin updates from the FCMs, followed the news, and communicated with OTC brokers like me via Instant Messenger; they were slowly being absorbed into the metastasizing e-commerce world. It was clear to everyone that the days of open outcry were numbered.

In 2013 the CME Group, which acquired the NYMEX-COMEX in 2008, sold its showpiece building to Brookfield Office Properties for $200 million. The CME was to remain in 449,000 square feet for two years and then shrink its presence by leasing 220,000 square feet for thirteen years thereafter. And then who knew?

The decline of the trading pits was a longer process than many of us, like Oscar, who declared the end of the floor was nigh back in 1992, expected, as the harbingers of the new age in trading emerged. Still, as CME Group chairman emeritus Leo Melamed once said, "Open outcry had no chance." And many floor traders now with no place to go would say with resignation as they left the business, "It was a great run." Forward thinkers like Leo, Oscar, and others read the tea leaves and moved to act as computerized trading came into its own. In the energy business, Enron made the first serious effort to supplant open outcry on the trading floor and voice brokering in the OTC markets with its Enron Online platform. Though the company eventually went under for reasons far removed from the trading floor, the concept was proven. By 2001, less than a decade after that first Globex print, 38 percent of natural gas trading was done online while the notional volume swelled from $50 billion in 2000 to $555 billion in 2001. At this same time, the fledgling Intercontinental Exchange entered the fray, picking up the e-baton left on the ground by the collapsed Enron. ICE now clears roughly six million futures and options contracts traded on its platform on an average daily basis.[10]

By 2010, 80 percent of CME's transactions moved through the Globex platform. In 2015, a spokesman for the CME effectively declared the end of open outcry. "Trading floor volumes for futures have been declining dramatically over the past five years, decreasing by 75 percent and now representing only one percent of the company's total futures volume. Our customers have overwhelmingly demonstrated, based on volumes, that they prefer electronic trading for futures. Keeping our floors open for the last several years has given customers time to adjust to this volume shift to the screen."[11] Such pronouncements accompanied CME's decision in July 2015 to dismantle half of its iconic Chicago trading pits.

In April 2016, an extraordinary if inevitable milestone in the evolution of finance was announced with very little fanfare or reflection. The CME Group declared it would shut down its New York City trading floor by the end of the year. By this time floor transactions represented just 0.3 percent of the overall energy and metals trading volume. Starting in January 2017, everything would be traded online and OTC. The closures left products listed at the company's NYMEX and COMEX exchanges available only for electronic trading. This development, along with CME's 2015 floor closures in Chicago,

---

10 Intercontinental Exchange, ADV 2022
11 "The Screen" is industry vernacular for electronic trading platforms.

effectively signaled the end of the raucous commodities pits that were a fixture in the American economic psyche since the Chicago Board of Trade launched the first futures exchange in 1848 ... thirteen years before the opening shots of the Civil War.

Today electronic platforms dominate a trading business that was once the exclusive domain of red-faced market-makers and brokers in the now-bygone trading pits. Shouts and phone calls and the *ka-chunk*! of stamping order tickets have been replaced with point-and-click; powerful algorithmic search engines scan the e-universe of financial transactions for the slightest pricing anomalies, seeking to pounce upon them with hyper speed and efficiency far beyond human capacity.

This shift to the screen was inevitable as online trading was more transparent and cheaper. And, to be blunt, OTC dealers no longer had the sneaking suspicion that they were the proverbial suckers at the table, selling something at X-1 here only to see someone else buy X+1 over there, whereas now on the screen it should, in theory at least, trade at the fair price of X. Admitted one former floor broker, with electronic trading "you could see whether you were getting ripped off or not." But, as long as there are markets there will be those who exploit whatever mechanism is used for transacting. The rise of high-frequency trading, for whom a microsecond was priceless, showed that what many perceived to be the unfair advantage of floor traders, who were able to get ahead of order flow as it hit the pits, has just been transferred to the world of software development and high-speed fiber optic cable. Indeed, as Edwin LeFèvre in his 1923 classic novel about trading, *Reminiscences of a Stock Operator*, reminds us: "There is nothing new on Wall Street."

There is a sense of loss, however, with the closing of the crowded trading floors. These bygone venues were the doorways through which those who might have lacked the proper pedigree, but did have innate intelligence, chutzpah, and work ethic, could enter what is now a very exclusive and high-credentialed professional space. As I have said, in the past "recruiting" often meant hiring the brother of a friend or taking a liking to some go-getter who sold you your only suit; often the path to success began as a clerk schlepping coffee for the traders in their colorful smocks and their overworked and underpaid yellowcoats.

The trading pits were the great equalizers. Today there is seemingly no place for the working-class kid willing to put in long hours for little pay to learn the art of trading through osmosis, as Oscar called it. Instead, the business is now the exclusive domain of those who hail from top-tier graduate schools offering advanced degrees in computer science, math, and high finance.

Beyond populist nostalgia, one must also wonder what is the loss to the world of derivatives itself when those who honed their acumen in the crucible of open outcry are shut out in favor of the Ivy League MBA. In the mind's eye, one can see a streetwise floor trader among the wizards at a hedge fund cautioning the quant magicians that what looks good on their models may not pan out in the real world of markets, as they are human constructs and thus do not always behave rationally. Markets, they might warn them, tend to remain unhinged longer than the rational can remain solvent, as those who were steamrolled by Brian Hunter, even though they turned out to be on the right side of his trades in the end, could attest. Those with the mindset of the fabled Mossad "tenth man," whose job it was to play devil's advocate and dissuade groupthink by imagining the unimaginable, many of whom were products of the trading pits, are fast becoming extinct. They have either left the business, as my brother and JEB eventually did, or are so removed from the trading desks that their input is more managerial than in making trading decisions. DAG, who now runs a global investing and trading enterprise, comes to mind.

Roger Lowenstein, in his book *When Genius Failed,* which detailed the rise and fall of LTCM—a hedge fund once lauded for its stable of quants, programmers, and even Nobel Prize–winning economists—illustrated the pitfalls of this trend well when he observed: "The professors had ignored the truism, of which they were well aware, that in markets the tails are always fat. Stuck in their glass-walled palace, far from New York's teeming trading floors, they had forgotten that traders were not random molecules, or even mechanical logicians…but people moved by greed and fear, capable of the extreme behavior and swings of mood so often observed in crowds…The professors hadn't modeled this. They'd programmed the market for a cold predictability that it had never had. They had forgotten the predatory, inquisitive, and overwhelmingly protective instincts that governed real-life traders. They'd forgotten the human factor."

With that said, the truly entrepreneurial OTC firms will continue to do well in the digital trading age. For those who are positioned on the right side of the technological divide one can even say this is an exciting period of innovation for commodities trading. Indeed, markets today are more transparent as traders can see real-time transactions all across the spectrum, allowing them to make more informed trading decisions. The massive exchange floors are a thing of the past...but platform execution, and the businesses that offer them, will grow and prosper because of the essential role they play in these unique but vital transactions.

For the rest, I can't see those with a more ossified mindset whom I'd watch stand helplessly in place as the floors were slowly pulled out from under them, and with no transferable skills other than being quick on their feet and good with numbers, and knowing when to "shut up and dance," surviving this new electronic age where entirely different, more analytical skills are essential to longevity. Oh well. As Judge Smails so coldly reminds us in *Caddyshack*: "The world needs ditch diggers too."

● ● ●

Commodities trading will continue to evolve hand in hand with technology. The modus operandi of open outcry on the tumultuous trading floor has been washed away like the handwriting on the sand before a rising tide. But for me the memories of what really was an extraordinary business, and the manner in which it was conducted, will remain. I see them as the purest expression of the markets as truly human systems. The screeching trader with flailing limbs frenetically scribbling on his little cards as the money flows through the phone lines surrounding the pits will be a mere rumor in the coming decades. But markets will always in the end be run by flawed, emotional, and often irrational human beings, and so the imprint of those moving money for reasons that do not always have a logic behind them will continue…and therefore so will opportunities to make one's fortune moving barrels of crude oil, molecules of natural gas, bushels of wheat and corn, ounces of silver and gold, money itself, or, should one wish to fantasize, frozen concentrated orange juice.

LeFèvre was right about there being nothing new on Wall Street. Because a market's underlying driving force, human beings, doesn't change, even if the technology does. Ultimately, a market is the amalgamation of millions of decisions by individuals—for every possible reason, be they grounded in cold logic or fevered emotion—that as a collective expression will push prices this way and that. And, often as not, no one will ever truly understand why. That is because people have been, and will always be, the same: brilliant and moronic, frugal and greedy, astute and tone-deaf, humble and arrogant, fearless and cowed, educated and ignorant. And the cowboy in them will continue to be drawn to the business that is the essence of capitalism stripped naked and raw. They will yearn to answer the simple question posed at the beginning of every trading day, whether the dealing commences with the banshee wail of a mosh futures pit, or the subdued point-and-click of the hedge fund manager in his secluded office: "Whaddya think here, up or down today?"

THE END

ACKNOWLEDGMENTS

THERE ARE SO MANY TO thank for bringing this book to your shelf, tablet, or headphones. I especially wish to acknowledge Anthony Ziccardi, president of Post Hill Press; Madeline Sturgeon, for her patience and pleasant demeanor during the editing process; and the good people at Simon & Schuster. And, of course, I'm grateful to my agent, Bob Thixton at Pinder Lane and Garon-Brooke, for his diligent advocacy on my behalf.

This book is not just my story. It belongs to all who gifted me with such fond recollections from my stint on the trading floors. The names and faces have stayed with me, along with the tinnitus and chronic sore back listed on the exchange invoice in return for my experiences. (Floor trading was indeed a contact sport.) In a popular television drama a while back, a character described our time on this earth as but a series of rooms, "and who we get stuck in those rooms with adds up to what our lives are." In the "room" that was my life in the final decade of the last century, I was stuck with many for whom I am grateful, not only for being the good friends and coworkers they were, but for teaching me the ways of both the trading profession and the wider business world. Wisdom surrounded me. And its purveyors were some of the most fascinating and truly bright people I have ever known. Among them were, in no particular order, Todd, Roger, Carolyn, Joe, several Mikes, Marks, Adams, and

Jeffs, Marco, Veck, Kevin, Norman, J. D., Jay, Bruce, Jimmy, Jerry, Marta, Ricky, Eric, Tina, Dean, Lucher, Ken, Bob, Rose, Andy, Kevin, Rich, and many others who gave me the impetus to write this book.

ABOUT THE AUTHOR

BRAD SCHAEFFER WAS A COMMODITIES options trader on the floors of the Chicago Mercantile Exchange and New York Mercantile Exchange as well as an equities trader on the American Stock Exchange. He now manages his own money trading over-the-counter. He is also a prolific author and columnist whose eclectic writings can be found on the pages of the *Wall Street Journal, New York Daily News, National Review,* The Federalist, Daily Wire, and ZeroHedge. He is the author of two acclaimed novels: the World War II drama *Of Another Time and Place* and bestseller *The Extraordinary,* which tackles autism and PTSD.